VENUS, MARS & VINO
"THE MODERN LOVE SURVIVOR'S GLOW & GROW GUIDE"

BY
ANNETTE MATTHEWS

Table of Contents

Foreword

*To every woman who ever mistook chaos
for connection, this one's for you.*

Welcome to **Venus, Mars & Vino: The Modern Love Survivor's
Glow & Grow Guide,** a book born somewhere between
heartbreak, healing,and a really good glass of wine.

If you've ever cried into your prosecco while declaring you're "so
done with dating," only to redownload the app three days later, this
book gets you.

If you've ever thought your love life needed divine intervention, a
therapist, or a group chat audit, you're in the right place.
And if you've ever looked in the mirror after a breakup and
whispered, *"I just want to feel like myself again,"* then, darling, this
one was written with you in mind.

Because this isn't a guide on how to find "the one."
It's a celebration of becoming *the one*, the version of yourself who
glows from self-respect, laughs at her own dating disasters, and
finally understands that peace is the real aphrodisiac.

When I started writing this book, I wasn't trying to create a dating
bible. I was trying to make sense of the chaos, the ghosters, the
gaslighters, the love-bombers, and yes, the exes who paid for
things they couldn't earn with integrity.

Somewhere between heartbreak and humour, I realised: surviving
modern love is less about finding answers and more about finding
yourself again, healed, hydrated, and hilariously self-aware.

Venus, Mars and Vino

Inside these pages, you'll find skincare routines that double as emotional resets, dating advice that feels like chatting with your most honest friend, and journal prompts that pull you back home to yourself. You'll also find stories, the messy, funny, empowering kind, because healing doesn't have to be heavy; sometimes it's just human.

So pour the vino, light the candle, and open your heart (and maybe your Notes app). You're about to rediscover that the best kind of glow-up isn't for a date, it's for your own damn reflection.

Because Venus may rule love, Mars may rule desire... but darling, you rule your own story now.

Here's to glowing, growing, and laughing your way through it all. One sip, one swipe, and one self-love ritual at a time.

Annette Matthews

Mum. Dental Hygienist. Skin Guru. Modern Love Survivor.

Dedication

For every woman who ever rebuilt herself between heartbreaks, this book is your mirror, your muse, and your permission slip to glow again.

For the ones who loved deeply, healed loudly,
and somehow kept their humour intact.
You are the story, the lesson, and the light.
Oh, and you are more than enough.

Here's to your comeback:
Equal parts chaos, courage, and a really good contour.

Annette xx

The Matador Moment
"To be honest, Annette… I'm not sure you're the best person to be giving advice-
AKA The Matador."

Jolene, my esteemed friend, ride-or-die, knows-too-much, wine companion, and part-time, actually full-time therapist.

Was she right? Maybe.
Did I run at red flags like they were a half-price sale?
Absolutely.

But that's exactly why this book exists.

Venus, Mars and Vino

For Lois

To my daughter Lois, my heart, my why, and the tiny powerhouse who once said:

"Mum, I nearly failed my GCSE English… how are you writing a whole book?"

Here's the truth, darling:
Because brilliance isn't measured in grades.
Because resilience beats perfection.
And because you and girls everywhere need to know you can build anything from courage, humour, and a little cosmic chaos.

You are limitless.
Keep shining.

For My Parents
To Mum and Dad

Thank you for cheering me on through every move, meltdown, glow-up and plot twist.

I left Derbyshire for a fresh start and probably have given you more issues than Vogue…
and yet you loved me, steadied me, and supported every chapter of this wild adventure.

I am who I am because of your strength, humour, and unwavering belief in me.

To My New Sisters Down Here

To the women who became my family in my new town
My unexpected soul sisters, hype team, emergency wine providers,
and the reason my outlook on life did a complete 180.

You showed me joy again.
You showed me laughter again.
You showed me, me again.

You are my girls for life. No
returns, no exchanges.

To the Old Friends, Colleagues & Lifelong Witnesses

To everyone who's known me through every era, the chaotic ones,
the romantic ones, the healing ones, and the ones best left off social
media…

Thank you for the support, the giggles, the "are you ok hun?"
messages,
and for laughing with me, not at me… though occasionally you did
both.

I know exactly who I am:
The girl you invite to the BBQ because you want belly-rolling
stories and guaranteed entertainment.

Thank you for loving me through it all.

Annette xxx

* * *

"Love letters became texts, glances became emojis, and somehow we still don't know what 'he's just busy' means."

The History of Dating – From Courtship to Casual

From Courtship to "Calling On"

In the 1800s, love was basically an administrative process. If you fancied someone, you didn't flirt or smile across them from the bar or coffee shop they didn't even exist (imagine), you called upon them in their family home, usually a friend of the family (maybe even a distant cousin, eek) or a suitor that had been hand selected for you, one of 'good stock' and suitably fertile to continue the family name.

That meant them turning up at the family home, potentially on a horse (supervised, of course), sitting in a parlour, and having polite conversation while everyone pretended not to be listening.

Sex before marriage? Absolutely not.
Emotional intimacy? Optional.
Dowry? Essential.

Women were prized for modesty, men for stability, and both for their ability to tolerate boredom.

If you were lucky, you got a few stolen glances before being married off like a Regency-era LinkedIn endorsement.

Venus, Mars and Vino

The Roaring Twenties – Dating Goes Public

Enter the jazz era, short skirts, and women who refused to
chaperone.
In the 1920s, "dating" became a public affair.
Literally, people went out.
Dancing, picnics, movies, maybe even a sneaky drink if you were
feeling totally scandalous.

For the first time, women had jobs, money, and would you believe
it, the audacity to choose who they wanted to see.
Men no longer "called on" women; they asked them out in person
or via telegram or letter (swoon)
Romantic autonomy was born, and so was the modern idea of
compatibility that maybe, just maybe, love should involve liking
each other.

The 1950s – Domestic Dreaming

The 'notebook' era, in which Ryan Gosling portrayed oh so well.

Their romance was initiated at this time, oh and a box of tissues is
required when watching!
We are referring to the post-war years, where everything was
painted in pastel optimism.
Love was sold in the packaging of picket fences, pressed shirts, and
perfectly set hair.
Dating was formal but fast; you met, you courted, you married, you
reproduced.
Conveyor belt dating.
Women were encouraged to "catch" a husband before 25 (heaven
forbid you became an "old maid")
Men were taught that emotional availability was for jazz musicians
and the French.

***

Still, there was charm in the simplicity of it all, no swiping, no "seen" messages or blue ticks, no existential dread about who else they're talking to and their fan list in the archive.
Just two people, a burger and a milkshake, and the illusion that forever was simple.
Think Grease, Danny and Sandy and Summer loving in tight leather leggings and leather jackets.

The 1960s–1970s – Free Love & Feminism

Think Austin Powers, floaty sleeves and flower power!
"Yeah, baby"
The sexual revolution blew the whole system wide open, and thank the Goddess of love for that.
The contraceptive pill arrived, women's rights gained ground, and suddenly love wasn't a one-way street to matrimony.

Dating became about self-discovery as much as romance.
Love was political, passionate, and personal.
People questioned monogamy, experimented with identity, and started seeing relationships as partnerships rather than property agreements or making babies to continue a family's heritage.

Of course, this was also when the "player" archetype entered pop culture, charming, detached, emotionally unavailable, and probably wearing flares, cue Austin Powers, again!
"Oh, behave!"

Venus, Mars and Vino

The 1980s–1990s – Love, Lust & your mum and dad's answering machines!

Cue shoulder pads, lip gloss, plucked and re-pencilled eyebrows, one shade of foundation and cassette tapes.
In the movies, there was also an awful lot of climbing out of windows to meet your man in their mode of transport!

Remember pausing and rewinding to record the lyrics on your cassette player, or was that just me…..That very process has given me an essential life skill and the ability to rap the whole of The Real Slim Shady.

Sitting with my Nokia 8210 playing Snake was my biggest worry back then.
The dating scene went cinematic, think When Harry Met Sally, Pretty Woman, and Sex and the City.

This was the era of personal ads ("SWF seeks kind, funny man who owns a sofa"), phone flirtations, and the beginning of "dating for fun" instead of "dating for forever."
Soul and soul mate searchin'

Relationships were becoming more egalitarian, but also more confusing.

The term "the one" was now part of the cultural script, which meant everyone was under pressure to find a soulmate with great hair and a decent sense of humour.

At the end of the nineties, MSN Messenger crept in, the first of the DMs.
Little did we know that in a few years this would be life …

The 2000s – Enter the Apps

Oh! And the millennials were born. Ah,

yes, the rise of the machines.
My Space crushes evolved into Tinder matches.
Suddenly, you could meet your next ex from the comfort of your
boujee couch.

Online dating shifted everything; love became a marketplace.
Profiles, bios, filters, and algorithms replaced basic face-to-face
human interaction.
It was liberating, but also overwhelming.
Instead of one "Mr Maybe," you had fifty "Mr Possibly-Nots"
waiting in your inbox.

The swiping culture gave us options, too many options and a
judgment call from just a profile picture of them holding a fish, a
mirror selfie or a flash of some abs from their own glow up in
2015.
Commitment became scarier, ghosting became easier, and
connection became, ironically, harder to find.

Venus, Mars and Vino

The 2010s–2020s – Conscious Uncoupling & Healing Eras

Welcome to the age of therapy, manifestation, and "doing the work." We now analyse our attachment styles like stock portfolios and know our Venus placements better than our postcodes, let's not even start on the super moon and its gravitational effects on individual mindsets.

We're redefining what dating even is. It's not just dinner and drinks anymore, it's energy alignment, it's trauma compatibility, it's "are you emotionally intelligent enough to text back in full sentences?"

We've gone from "till death do us part" to "till personal growth makes us incompatible." But maybe that's okay.

The Present Day – Dating in the Wild Wild West- The cowgirl element will be relevant later in the book!
Now, in the 2020s, we're living in the most paradoxical dating era of all time.
We crave intimacy but fear vulnerability. We talk about connection but swipe past it.
We ghost people while posting self-love quotes.

And yet, amidst all the chaos, there's hope because at its core, dating hasn't changed all that much.
It's still about searching for connection, understanding ourselves through others, and finding that spark that makes us feel alive again.
The best version of ourselves.

***

The settings have changed, the dance floors are digital, the love letters are DMs, and the heartbreaks arrive via notification, but the heart? Still the same old troublemaker.

Coming up next: we'll ask the million-pound question, what even is love?
Spoiler: it's not just butterflies.
It's biology, brain chemistry, and occasionally, bad decisions.

"Love is like a good bottle of wine, it starts with butterflies, ends with overthinking, and somewhere in the middle you convince yourself it's 'meant to be.'"

What Is Love, Anyway?

Love

The word that's launched a thousand rom-coms, several divorces,
and at least three Adele albums.
We all claim to know what it feels like that warm, fuzzy, everything-
is-sparkly sensation, but try to define it, and suddenly you sound
like a teenage dirtbag in some sort of crisis.

So… what *is* love, exactly?
Is it chemistry?
Compatibility?
Shared trauma and a Netflix password and or matching dry
robes…?

Let's unpack it… heart first, science second.

The Three-Part Recipe for Love

Love is part biology, part psychology, and part mystery.
You can't logic your way into it, but you can understand why your
brain behaves like it's on drugs when you fall into it.

1. **Lust:** That primal, hormonal "who is that?" moment. It's all
testosterone, oestrogen, and pheromones, nature's way of
shouting,
"Mate now, think later."

* * *

2. **Attraction:** The dopamine and adrenaline cocktail that turns you into an obsessed, smiling fool who suddenly enjoys their phone sounding off every three minutes.

3. **Attachment:** The calmer phase — oxytocin and serotonin take over, and you feel safe, bonded, and mildly co-dependent in a cute way.

Basically, your brain is a chemical rave that slowly turns into a cuddle puddle.

The Psychology of Why We Fall

Science says love often begins with recognition.
We're drawn to what feels familiar, even if it's not always good for us. Ever dated someone who felt "like home" and then realised "home" was a bit of a mess?
Yeah, that.

We subconsciously seek partners who mirror our earliest emotional experiences, the good, the bad, and the slightly traumatic.
Freud would have a field day with your dating history.

Love, then, is not always the universe sending you your soulmate.
Sometimes it's actually your nervous system trying to finish old business in a new relationship.
The term gut instinct…. That's what we are talking about here…

Lust vs Love vs Attachment: The Eternal Mix-Up

Think of it this way:

* * *

Stage	Feels Like	Looks Like	Lasts How Long
Lust	Fireworks	Intense texting, sexy selfies	6 weeks–3 months
Love	Connection	Deep talks, vulnerability, future fantasies	6 months–forever
Attachment	Safety	Shared routines, quiet comfort	The long game

The Brain on Love: A Comedy of Chemicals

Falling in love literally messes with your brain.
Dopamine spikes, cortisol drops, and rational thought take a little holiday.
That's why your best friend sounds deranged explaining how their new boyfriend "isn't like the others" (A little heads up: he probably is).

MRI studies show that the brain of someone newly in love looks suspiciously similar to the brain of someone on cocaine.
Which explains a lot of the euphoria, the obsession, the poor decision-making.

So when your mates say, "You're addicted to him," they're not wrong.
You kind of are.

Venus, Mars and Vino

The Cultural Madness of Modern Love

We've turned love into a job description.
You're supposed to find someone who's your best friend, therapist, gym buddy, travel partner, and twin flame, all while maintaining perfect skin and boundaries.

Modern dating culture sells love as both the ultimate freedom and the ultimate security.
It's confusing.
We want adventure and safety, sparks and calm, chaos and peace.
Basically, we want a walking paradox with a stable attachment style and a love language we can comprehend.

The Truth No One Wants to Admit

Love isn't always butterflies and fireworks.
Sometimes it's showing up tired, annoyed, and still choosing each other.
It's patience, kindness, accountability and the ability to say "sorry" without turning it into a hostage negotiation.

Love, at its healthiest, is less about losing yourself in someone and more about finding a home within yourself, then inviting someone to visit without redecorating everything for them.

***

Love in the Modern Era: The Self-Love Revolution

Here's the twist: before you can love them, you have to LOVE
YOURSELF
Not the "bubble bath and affirmations" kind (though those are nice),
but the deep, honest, "I know my worth and my wounds" kind.
Because healed love hits different, it's not desperate; it's
deliberate. It's two whole people choosing to share a life, not two
broken ones trying to glue each other back together.

So, what is love?

It's more than a feeling, it's an action, a choice, and sometimes, a
beautifully chaotic act of courage.

And now that we've defined it (loosely, poetically, and with
science), let's see how we speak it.

Let us explore where we pit Love Languages vs Star Signs and find
out why your Capricorn ex never said "I love you" but showed up
with a spreadsheet instead.

"Love is the only thing that makes perfectly sane people write paragraphs, delete them, then send 'ok.'"

Love Languages vs Star Signs: Speak My Love or Read My Chart

The Five Love Languages: Gary Chapman's Emotional IKEA Manual

Dr Gary Chapman gave us the five love languages back in the 90s, and honestly, it's the best relationship cheat sheet since vino and apologies.

They're basically the user manual for how you give and receive love, the romantic equivalent of "some assembly required."

***

Here's the breakdown:

1. *Words of Affirmation: You need to hear love.*
Compliments, encouragement, and "I'm proud of you" make your heart melt faster than a candle in Ibiza.
Dating downside: You might overthink every text.
Signature phrase: "You haven't said you love me today…"

2. *Acts of Service: You show love by doing things*
Fixing the Wi-Fi, making coffee, remembering the car's MOT. It's not sexy, but it's solid.
Dating downside: You get stuck mothering your partner.
Signature phrase: "I did your washing"

3. *Receiving Gifts: Not to be confused with gold-digging.*
For you, thoughtful presents = proof of affection.
A daisy picked from a garden says more than a diamond from guilt.
Dating downside: You can't hide your disappointment when they forget an anniversary.
Signature phrase: "It's not about the gift, it's about *the meaning."

4. *Quality Time: You crave undivided attention.*
No phones, no distractions, just being together, ideally somewhere with cocktails, candlelight and eye contact.
Dating downside: You'll start a fight over them scrolling mid-date.
Signature phrase: "Are you even listening… or scrolling?"

5. *Physical Touch: You're fluent in cuddles.*
A brush of the arm, a morning kiss, a leg touch under the table, that's yourlove currency.
Dating downside: You feel rejected when they forget to hold your hand. Signature phrase: "You haven't hugged me in an hour. Are we okay?"

Star Signs: The Celestial Soap Opera

Now, onto astrology. The ancient art of blaming our emotional chaos on planets.

Whether you're a loyal Taurus or a flighty Gemini, your star sign supposedly shapes how you love, fight, and flirt. It's psychology meets sparkle.

Let's decode the zodiac's dating personalities….

♈ Aries (March 21–April 19): Passionate, bold, impulsive. Will fall in love before they know your surname.
Loses interest if you take too long to text back.

♉ Taurus (April 20–May 20): Loyal, stubborn, and sensual. Loves comfort and routine.
Won't forgive easily, unless there's food.

♊ Gemini (May 21–June 20): Witty, restless, and slightly chaotic. They'll charm your socks off, then ghost you because they got distracted by a new podcast.

♋ Cancer (June 21–July 22): Sensitive and nurturing.
Loves hard, cries harder.
Will bake you lasagne and analyse your childhood trauma by week two.

♌ Leo (July 23–August 22): Glamorous and generous.
Needs attention like oxygen.
If you forget to compliment their outfit, they'll assume you've fallen out of love.

***

Venus, Mars and Vino

♍ Virgo (August 23–September 22): Analytical, dependable, and slightly allergic to feelings.
Will love you practically, spreadsheets, reminders, and all.

♎ Libra (September 23–October 22): Charming, flirty, and indecisive.
Will make you feel adored, then vanish mid-argument because "conflict ruins my aura."

♏ Scorpio (October 23–November 21): Intense, loyal, mysterious.
They'll either be your soulmate or your most unforgettable mistake. Sometimes both.

♐ Sagittarius (November 22–December 21): Adventurous, hilarious, allergic to commitment.
Will book a flight or an Uber mid-argument, Yep, That's me!

♑ Capricorn (December 22–January 19): Ambitious, grounded, emotionally constipated. Shows love by fixing your taxes and judging your budgeting.

♒ Aquarius (January 20–February 18): Quirky, intellectual, and emotionally unavailable in a charming way.
Will talk about space but not their feelings.

♓ Pisces (February 19–March 20): Dreamy, empathetic, slightly delusional.
Will write you poetry and then cry when you don't get it.
Venus, Mars and Vino

When Love Languages and Star Signs Collide

Think of it like this: your love language is your hardware, and your star sign is your software.

The two together explain everything, including why your Virgo boyfriend cleans the kitchen instead of saying "I love you."

Here's how they often overlap:

Star Sign	Likely Love Language	Example of Love Gone Right	Example of Love Gone Wrong
Aries	Physical Touch	Passionate, exciting chemistry	Impulsive flings, burns fast
Taurus	Acts of Service	Breakfast in bed, long cuddles	Refuses to compromise
Gemini	Words of Affirmation	Flirty banter, endless talk	Emotional inconsistency
Cancer	Quality Time	Netflix & nurture	Smothering levels of attention
Leo	Words of Affirmation	Grand gestures & praise	Sulks when ignored
Virgo	Acts of Service	Thoughtful support	Feels unappreciated
Scorpio	Gifts & Words	Romance & aesthetics	Can't decide what they want
Sagittarius	Quality Time	Deep connection	Jealousy & secrecy
Capricorn	Acts of Service	Dependable love	Emotionally distant
Aquarius	Independence & quality time	Consistent and mutual	Keeps you guessing

Venus, Mars and Vino

So Which One Matters More?

Honestly, both. Love languages tell you how to communicate love. Star signs hint at how you express it.

Knowing both is like switching on the lights in a room you've been stumbling around for years. You suddenly get why your Scorpio ex needed reassurance while your Sagittarius fling bolted at the mention of feelings.

It's not about excusing behaviour, it's about understanding patterns, so you stop repeating the same emotional carnage with a different zodiac sign.

The Real Lesson

At the end of the day, whether you're fluent in "Acts of Service" or born under a dramatic Leo moon, love works best when both people actually listen to one another.

No chart, quiz, or compatibility calculator can replace honesty, effort, and empathy.

So yes, check your birth chart, but also check your communication. Read their stars, but read their actions louder.

Because true compatibility isn't written in the sky. It's written in how you show up every day, texts, touches, time, and trust.

Next up: we're firing off into cosmic chemistry itself.

Venus & Mars – Why We Date Like We're From Different Planets.
***

A note from Annette*: It's not just about gender.*
It's about energy, ego, and the cosmic dance between desire and independence.

Venus, Mars and Vino

"Venus wants connection, Mars wants directions, and neither one reads the emotional GPS."

Venus & Mars: Why We Date Like We're From Different Planets

Venus: The Goddess of Love (and Long Voice Notes)

Venus energy is all about attraction, connection, and beauty.
It's soft, emotional, magnetic the pull rather than the push.
People with strong Venus energy are the ones who:

Remember your birthday and your rising sign.
Think foreplay starts with conversation.
Can sense a mood shift faster than dips in wifi connection.

Venus is love as art. She's/He's the side of us that nurtures, receives, and creates harmony.
She/He craves intimacy, reassurance, and romance that feels safe enough to unfold.

But here's the catch, Venus energy can easily slip into over-giving, overthinking, and romantic over investment.
She's/He's the one waiting for the text that doesn't come, writing novels in her/his head about what went wrong.

Mars: The God of Drive (and Selective Hearing)

Mars energy is direct, bold, and forward-moving.
It's the spark that says, "Let's do something about it," rather than, "Let's talk about how we feel."
People with strong Mars energy tend to:

Text first, plan the date, and drive the car.
Handle conflict like a competitive sport.
- Be passionate one minute and emotionally MIA the next.
***

Venus, Mars and Vino

Mars is action, pursuit, and clarity, but when unchecked, it can also be impatient, defensive, or dismissive.
Mars energy loves to win. And sometimes, that means avoiding vulnerability because it feels like losing control.

Men are from Mars, Women are from Venus. (Bullsh!t)

🤜 When the Woman Is "Mars"

She tends to be:

- **Goal-oriented and independent.** She likes solving problems herself and values results over process.

- **Direct in communication.** She says what she means, may prefer concise or practical conversations.

- **Action-focused.** When facing stress, she might withdraw to think or do something to fix it rather than talk it out.

- **Emotionally self-contained.** She may not share feelings until she's processed them privately.

🤝 When the Man Is "Venus"

He tends to be:

- **Emotionally expressive.** He values talking about feelings and connection.

- **Empathetic and supportive.** He seeks harmony and often prioritises the relationship's emotional atmosphere.

- **Relationally focused.** He might need verbal reassurance or closeness to feel secure.

- **Collaborative.** He tends to look for shared understanding rather than competition or problem-solving.

The Cosmic Dance: Why We're Drawn to Our Opposite Energy

In relationships, Venus and Mars energies are constantly doing a pushpull tango.
Venus attracts; Mars pursues. Venus softens; Mars strengthens. Venus feels; Mars acts.

That polarity that tantric tension is what creates chemistry.
Without it, love can feel flat.
Too much of it, and we get drama.

It's why opposites attract: we're all subconsciously seeking some sort of balance.
The emotional one wants grounding; the stoic one wants warmth.
The planner needs spontaneity; the free spirit craves stability.

We're not just dating people; we're dating their energy systems.

The Gender Myth (and the Modern Rewrite)

Old-school dating advice painted men as hunters and women as gatherers, but honestly?

That's ancient history.
Today, Venus and Mars energies live in everyone.

You can be a fiercely independent woman with strong Mars energy who still melts when someone brings her coffee in bed.
Or a sensitive, intuitive man with Venus energy who leads with empathy and still gets the job done.

Healthy relationships aren't about conforming to gender scripts they're about balancing both energies.

Too much Mars, and you burn out or bulldoze.
Too much Venus, and you lose yourself trying to please.

***

Venus, Mars and Vino

When Venus and Mars Collide (a.k.a. Texting Misunderstandings 101

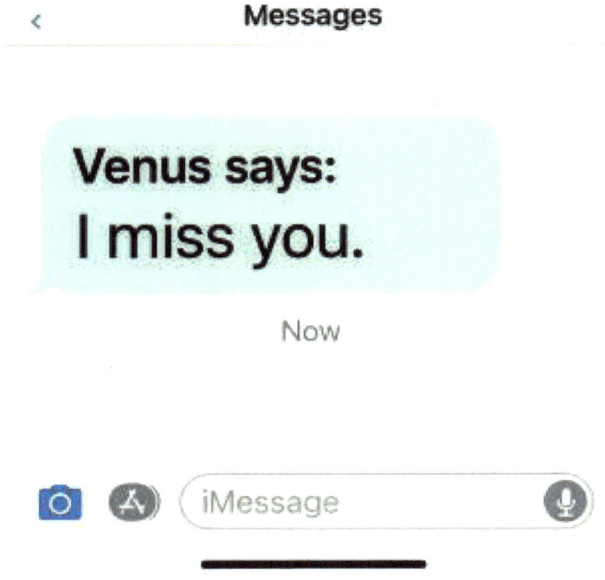

Mars hears: "She/he's needy."

Mars says:
I'm busy.

Now

iMessage

Venus hears: *"He/she's not interested."*

Venus wants: Emotional connection.
Mars wants: Problem-solving.

Venus overthinks: Every emoji.
Mars overestimates: His/Her communication skills.

See the issue? Both mean well, they're just speaking different emotional languages.
Mars moves, Venus feels. Mars fixes, Venus flows.

The magic happens when each learns to do a little of both.
When Venus learns to say, "Here's what I need," without apology.
When Mars learns to listen without feeling like they are under attack.

Venus, Mars and Vino

Finding Balance: Integrating Venus and Mars

The healthiest relationships don't suppress one side -they synchronise
them.
Here's how that looks in practice:

For the Venusians: Don't dim your emotional intelligence - just set
boundaries with it.
You can care deeply without caretaking everyone's feelings.

For the Martians: Don't hide behind logic.
Strength isn't about stoicism, it's about being secure enough to be seen,
feelings and all.

When Venus and Mars meet halfway, love feels like flow and fire,
calm but exciting, steady but sexy.

Pop Culture Exhibit A: Carrie and Big (a Venus-Mars Tragedy)

Carrie Bradshaw, pure Venus. Romantic, intuitive, dramatic.
Mr. Big, all Mars. Controlled, detached, allergic to emotional clarity.

Their chemistry was undeniable, their timing always tragic.
Venus kept hoping Mars would open up; Mars kept hoping Venus would
stop overanalysing.
They mirrored what so many of us go through: the tug between wanting
love and fearing surrender.

If they'd both done a bit of healing? Venus could've kept her sparkle
without chasing validation, and Mars could've stayed powerful without
running.

Moral of the story: cosmic chemistry is great however emotional
maturity wins every time.

***

So, Who's Driving the Spaceship?
In an ideal world, Venus and Mars work as co-pilots, ready Maverick?

Venus says, "Let's connect."
Mars says, "Let's make it happen."

Together, they create relationships that feel balanced, the warmth of love with the thrill of desire.

Because when Venus and Mars stop fighting and start flirting, love stops being a battlefield and starts being an adventure.

Next up: we'll look at why opposites attract (until they don't) the magnetism of difference, the pitfalls of polarity, and how to tell whether your relationship is fated… or just fiery.

"They say opposites attract, which must be why I keep pulling in emotionally unavailable men like I'm a magnet for mayhem."

Opposites Attract (Until They Don't)

Why We're Wired for the Opposite
Would you see a Viking dating a cowgirl?
That would be a power couple, right there.

Humans are hardwired to seek balance.
It's nature's way of making sure we don't all live identical lives in
matching cardigans.

Psychologically speaking, we're drawn to traits we lack or
suppress. Your confident partner might embody the boldness you
secretly crave. Their independence might mirror the autonomy you
wish you had.

It's an attraction as compensation, your unconscious saying,
"Yes, that one, they have something you need to learn."

And oh, learn you will.
Usually, through tears, growth, and a few "I can fix them" speeches,
your friends have heard way too many times.

***

The Fireworks Phase: When Opposites Feel Magical

At the start, opposites are perfect.
You fill each other's gaps like a romantic 5000-piece jigsaw puzzle.

You're steady; they're wild.
You ground them; they lift you.
You love routines; they love surprises.

Together, you're a Netflix original waiting to happen.

Every difference feels exciting, a window into another world.
You marvel at how they live so freely, how they make choices
without consulting five group chats.
You feel alive.

That's the honeymoon high: difference feels like discovery.

The Reality Check: When "Opposite" Starts Feeling Like "Obstacle"

Then… the shine starts to fade.
The quirks that once made your heart race now make your eye
twitch.

The "free spirit" who once inspired you now just forgets to text
back. The "calm and grounded" partner now feels emotionally
distant. The "ambitious go-getter" has turned into someone who
can't switch off work for date night.

What was once complementarity turns into conflict.
You start trying to convert each other, gently at first, then with the
emotional persistence of a self-help cult.

Opposites may attract, but they also exhaust.

Chemistry vs Compatibility: The Cruel Trick

Here's the uncomfortable truth: Chemistry isn't compatibility.

Chemistry is electricity.
Compatibility is wiring.

You can have sparks that light up the sky, but if the circuits aren't built to handle it, eventually something blows.

Compatibility is about values, communication, and life rhythm.
Do you want the same things?
Do you handle stress similarly?
Are you both emotionally available on the same schedule?

Opposites can fall madly in love.
But if they don't respect each other's core needs, that passion turns into polarity and not the sexy kind.

The "You Complete Me" Myth

Hollywood sold us a lie: that we're half-people wandering around waiting for someone to complete us.
In reality, relationships work best when two whole people choose to share space, not fill gaps.

When we chase our opposites from a place of lack, hoping they'll balance us out, we end up codependent.
You become the caretaker, they become the chaos, and neither of you gets to grow.

The goal isn't to find someone who completes you.
It's to find someone who complements you without erasing yourself in the process.

Learning From Your Opposite

Here's the thing: every opposite comes bearing a gift.
The loud one teaches you to speak up.
The quiet one teaches you to listen.
The planner shows the dreamer how to build.
The dreamer shows the planner how to breathe.

The trick is to *learn* from each other without trying to *become* each other.

If you can integrate their lessons without losing your balance, you win. If not, you'll keep playing emotional tennis until someone storms off the court.

When It's Worth Fighting For

Not all opposite pairings are doomed;
some are downright legendary.
The key is emotional maturity and shared values.
If your communication styles differ but your intentions align,
you can bridge that gap.
If your goals are the same but your approaches vary,
you can meet in the middle.

The difference that kills relationships isn't personality,
it's lack of emotional effort.
Opposites can attract for a lifetime when both are willing to grow
towards each other rather than away.

***

Red Flags Masquerading as "Opposite Energy"

Let's clear something up: being emotionally unavailable, inconsistent, or chaotic isn't "mysterious opposite energy." It's just bad behaviour.

If you're rationalising toxicity as "we're just really different," please step away from the flame.
Opposites attract, but you don't need to burn.

Remember: passion without peace is just adrenaline dressed up as love.

The Sweet Spot: Complementary, Not Conflicting

The magic happens when you meet someone who challenges you *without* destabilising you.
They bring out your edges, not your anxiety.
They stretch your comfort zone without shredding your boundaries.

That's when opposites evolve from a crash course into a partnership.
You learn from each other, grow together, and find the balance between spark and sanity.

Because yes, opposites attract, but it's the ones who learn how to align that actually last.

Next up: we dive into The Rules of Attraction, the science, the energy, and the subtle signals that make us swipe right, fall hard, and sometimes run fast.

A note from Annette: it's not just about looks (don't roll your eyes at me! it's not!) It's about confidence, connection, and chemistry that doesn't self-destruct.

"The rules of attraction are simple: smell good, text back, and don't be emotionally unavailable."

The Rules of Attraction: Why We Want Who We Want

The Science Bit: Attraction by Design

Your brain is sneaky.
When you meet someone new, it runs a silent background check that includes smell, sound, symmetry, and something called genetic complementarity.

Basically, your body is trying to build the best possible future offspring without asking your opinion.

Here's the cheat sheet:

Scent: You're more likely to be drawn to someone whose natural body chemistry signals genetic diversity.
Translation: if you like how they smell when they're slightly sweaty, you're doomed.

Symmetry: Evolution loves balance.
Facial symmetry is often linked to health, which your subconscious translates as
"Yes, mate, now."

Voice: Studies show women are drawn to deeper voices and men to higher-pitched ones, both subconsciously linked to fertility cues.
Romantic, right?

Pheromones: They're real, invisible, and wildly unhelpful when you're trying to stop fancying someone toxic.
Basically, attraction starts before your brain gets a vote.

The Psychological Side: Familiar Feels Safe

You might think you're picking partners based on charm, wit, and how well they quote Friends, Let's Pivot!
In reality, your subconscious is scanning for familiarity.

Your early experiences, how love felt, how attention was given or withheld, from your "attraction template."

So if your parents were distant, chaotic, or overbearing, guess what?
You're likely to chase someone who triggers the same emotional dynamic.
It feels familiar, not necessarily good.

That's why we often confuse intensity for intimacy.
The adrenaline rush of anxiety feels like chemistry, when it's really just your nervous system mistaking stress for excitement.

The Confidence Code

Forget abs and perfect hair, confidence is the real aphrodisiac.
Confidence says, "I know who I am."
Neediness says, "Please tell me who I am."

We're instinctively drawn to people who seem comfortable in their own skin because it signals emotional safety and self-sufficiency.
That doesn't mean arrogance (a tragic epidemic on dating apps).
True confidence is quiet, calm, and grounded.
It's someone who doesn't need to dominate the room; they own their energy without shouting about it.

Confidence whispers; insecurity screams.

Energy Chemistry: Vibes Don't Lie

Attraction isn't just physical, it's energetic.
Ever met someone who didn't tick any of your boxes but instantly felt magnetic?
That's frequency alignment.

Every human emits a subtle energy signature, a mix of their mood, mindset, and self-worth. When two energies match, it feels like fireworks.
When they don't, it feels like forcing a Wi-Fi connection that just won't stick.

It's why timing matters.
The same person can feel irresistible when you're open and healed or completely wrong when you're insecure and searching.

Sometimes, attraction isn't about *them* at all.
It's about where *you* are vibrationally.

The Red Flag Illusion

You know those people who make you feel alive and a little bit insane?
Yeah, that's not chemistry, that's chaos disguised as passion.

There's a fine line between "we have undeniable chemistry" and "my nervous system is in fight-or-flight, but make it sexy."

Real attraction feels exciting and safe.
You can breathe.
You don't have to overperform or overthink.
You feel pulled toward them, but you're still yourself.

If you have to shrink to keep someone's interest, that's not attraction, that's survival.

Venus, Mars and Vino

Why Timing is Everything

Attraction is often less about who you meet and more about when you Venus, Mars and Vino meet them.

Ever notice how you suddenly find stable people attractive after therapy or a period of self-healing?
Or how emotionally unavailable types lose their sparkle once you've healed your abandonment issues?
That's because attraction evolves with self-awareness.

Your energy dictates your dating pool.
When you're in chaos, you attract chaos.
When you're grounded, you attract calm.

So before you go looking for "the one," make sure you're someone worth finding.

The Rule of The Magnetic Mirror

Here's the spiritual kicker: people you're strongly drawn to are often mirrors.
They reflect back what you need to see, your desires, your fears, your patterns.

The charming commitment-phobic might be showing you your fear of rejection.
The emotionally unavailable hottie could be highlighting where you withhold love from yourself.

Attraction isn't random. It's a compass pointing toward your next lesson.

The question is, are you learning, or just repeating?

How to Keep the Spark Without the Car Crash

Sustaining attraction long-term takes intention.
Here's how:

1. Stay curious.
Familiarity kills excitement; keep rediscovering each other.

2. Balance independence and intimacy. Space makes the heart grow fonder and saner.

3. Keep your polarity alive.
A little difference keeps things spicy, just not toxic.

4. Grow together. Attraction thrives on admiration. Keep evolving, individually and as a pair.

The real secret?
Attraction that lasts isn't about perfection; it's about evolution.

The Bottom Line

Attraction is both mystery and a mirror, biology, psychology, and a dash of cosmic irony.
We fall for people who reflect our energy, challenge our comfort zones, and teach us what we still need to heal.

It's never random. It's rarely rational. And it's always revealing. Because the true rule of attraction isn't just about finding someone who excites you, it's about becoming someone you're excited to be with.

Next up: We'll unpack Personality Traits & the People We Pick.

Why we keep dating the same archetypes, how attachment styles sneak into our love lives, and how to finally break the pattern without breaking your heart.

"Love is basically emotional karaoke, everyone's winging it, some sound great, and others shouldn't have tried."

Personality, Patterns & the People We Pick

Personality: The Spark and the Safety Blanket

Your personality type influences what you find attractive and what drives you absolutely mad.

If you're logical and cautious, you might crave someone spontaneous to loosen you up.
If you're nurturing and empathetic, you might gravitate toward people who need care.
(High five to those with codependent tendencies and the forever giving empaths).

If you're ambitious and driven, you might fancy someone who reminds you to chill the hell out.

We don't just date who we like.
We date those who help us balance ourselves, consciously or not.

But when balance turns into dependence, that's when we start mistaking emotional work for emotional connection.

The Big Five Personality Traits and Their Dating Habits

Let's do a quick science meets reality tour of the 'Big Five' personality traits, with a sprinkling of rom-com wisdom:

***

THE BIG 5

PERSONALITY TRAITS & DATING VIBES

Trait	The Good	The Challenge	THEIR DATING VIBE
Openness	Adventurous, creative, curious	Commitment-phobic when bored	"Let's move to Bali and start a podcast."
Conscientiousnes	Reliable, organised, thoughtful	Can be rigid or controlling	"I made us a colour-code Google calendar."
Extraversion	Energetic, social, expressive	Easily distracted, needs attention	"We're going to three parties tonight."
Agreeabeleness	Kind, empathetic, cooperative	Avoids conflict at all costs	"No, it's finel I love being ignored!"
Neuroticism	Deeply emotional, intuitive	Anxiety-ridden, overthinks everything	"Are you mad at me? You took 14. minutes to reply."

In healthy combinations, these traits complement each other.

But mix too much of one with too little of another, and your relationship dynamic becomes a group project where only one person's doing the legwork

45

Attachment Styles: The Invisible Blueprint

Now, let's get into the psychology of love patterns and the theory of attachment.

This is the stuff that explains why one person panics when you don't text back, another vanishes after three great dates, and someone else somehow manages to stay chill.

There are four main attachment styles:

1. Secure: Comfortable with intimacy and independence.
Communicates well.
Rare unicorn.

2. Anxious: Craves closeness but fears rejection. Overthinks everything.

3. Avoidant: Values independence, fears dependence. Great at disappearing mid-conversation.

4. Disorganised (Fearful-Avoidant): The emotional rollercoaster, wants love desperately but also fears it.
Will both chase and run!

We often end up pairing anxious and avoidant types; it's the cosmic irony of dating.
One wants to merge, the other wants to hide.
It's basically an emotional tag with kissing and 'stuff!'

***

The Cycle: Familiar Pain Feels Like Passion

Here's the cruel joke: your subconscious isn't looking for happiness, it's looking for familiarity.

If love felt inconsistent when you were young, inconsistency will feel Venus, Mars and Vino like home.
If love were conditional, you'd mistake earning affection for intimacy.
If love were chaotic, calm would feel boring until you realise peace is just passion without panic.

We don't repeat patterns because we're masochists. We repeat them because we're trying to resolve them.

The universe keeps sending you the same lesson in a different body until you finally graduate.

The Archetypes We Can't Stop Dating

You've met these people, and maybe been them.
The Fixer: "I can help them change." Polite note: you can't.

The Mystery: Emotionally distant, perpetually intriguing.

Never fully present.

The Caretaker: Over-giver, under-receiver.

Thinks love equals service.

The Rebel: Wild, magnetic, allergic to plans.

The Rock: Dependable, safe… sometimes too safe.

The Mirror: Feels like fate because they reflect your unhealed parts

right back at you.

***

It can be referred to as a 'Twin flame,' but that's a whole new subject in its entirety.

You're not cursed if you keep attracting the same type. You're simply being invited to heal what that type triggers in you.

Breaking the Pattern

Step one: awareness, open your eyes and your mind!
You can't fix what you don't see.
Once you start recognising your emotional autopilot, you can finally override it.

Step two: slow down, easy tiger!
Attraction that feels like lightning might be chemistry, or it might just be your trauma saying, "Oh, hello again."

Step three: date from your healed self, not your hungry self.
Your healed self says, "I want to connect." Your hungry self says, "I need to be chosen."

One builds love. The other builds cycles.

The Healed Attraction Test

Ask yourself before you fall in (or back into) something:

Do I feel safe being myself around this person?
Do they communicate consistently, even when it's not convenient?
Do I feel grounded, not anxious, when I'm with them?
Does the connection grow through clarity, not chaos?

If yes, congratulations, you might be entering your healed dating era.

If no, maybe skip the situation-ship sequel.

Venus, Mars and Vino

When Patterns Become Preferences

Healing doesn't mean your "type" disappears.
It just means your type evolves.
Instead of chasing adrenaline, you start craving alignment. Instead
of obsessing over attention, you seek consistency.
You realise peace isn't boring, it's the most seductive thing there is.

Because healed love doesn't need drama to feel alive.
It just needs truth.

*Next up: We're turning our eyes (and our hearts) to the stars: Star
Signs & Sex Appeal, where we decode who turns us on, who turns
us off, and which zodiac signs are most likely to send "you up?"
texts at 2 a.m.*

"Astrology doesn't lie; some people are born to seduce, and others are just here to emotionally confuse the rest of us."

Star Signs & Sex Appeal: The Cosmic Chemistry of Dating

(Because sometimes the stars explain what the group chat can't.)

We've all been there, halfway through a date, sipping a cocktail, when something feels *off.*
He's charming, funny, a little mysterious… but also *emotionally allergic to vulnerability.*

Cue your best friend whispering: *"What's his star sign?"*

Welcome to the zodiac of modern dating, where cosmic chemistry meets human chaos.

But here's the thing: astrology isn't just about guessing who's good in bed or who texts back slowly
(though… it's definitely part of the fun).
It's a language of *energy.*
A way to understand *why* we connect, *how* we love, and *what* makes us feel desired, safe, or seen.

The Cosmic Love Equation

If love languages are the *vocabulary* of affection, then astrology is the *accent.*
It's the rhythm behind our romance, the reason one person makes your heart race while another feels like home.

And when it comes to sex appeal? That's where the planets start flirting.
***

- **Venus** whispers how you attract and express love, your romance radar.
  - **Mars** dictates your passion, drive, and turn-ons, your *raw energy.*

Together, they choreograph your chemistry, whether it's instant magnetism or a slow-burn connection that sneaks up on you during a Sunday brunch. (Not the bottomless kind!)

Love, Lust & Lessons from the Zodiac

Each sign carries its own sensual signature.
Aries brings fire, Taurus brings touch, Gemini brings curiosity, and so on.

But beyond the memes and the astrology apps, there's something deeper here: a mirror into our emotional DNA.

Understanding your sign (and your partner's) doesn't mean predicting destiny; it means decoding *dynamics.*
Because when you understand what ignites someone's energy, you stop taking things personally and start seeing patterns.

The hot-and-cold text guy? Probably an Aquarius.
The overly intense first-dater? Scorpio with a Venus in Pisces, obviously!

From the Stars to the Everyday

Here's the cosmic truth: your sign doesn't just influence how you date, it shapes how you live.
How you rest.
Eat. Connect. Nurture.
Even how you care for your pets, check out my bonus content with my mini pet energy and astrology guide in the next section!

Why We Look to the Stars for Love

Astrology is basically personality psychology with better accessories.

While psychologists have the Big Five, which we have covered in the last chapter, astrology has the Big Twelve, archetypes representing different emotional needs and expressions.

Astrology helps us understand why we're drawn to some people and baffled by others. It's not about "good" or "bad" matches, it's about energy compatibility.

Because sometimes, it's not that he's ghosting you, it's that his Venus is in Aquarius and emotional detachment is his love language.

The Elements of Attraction

Each sign falls into one of four elements, and these elements are the
real chemistry test.

🔥Fire Signs (Aries, Leo, Sagittarius- that's me!) Passionate,
impulsive, magnetic.
They love the chase and the drama.
Attraction for them is a sport, not a destination.
Warning: They burn bright, but sometimes short.

Dating one (apparently) feels like: Being on a rollercoaster
blindfolded after a bottle of wine and a cheeseboard, thrilling,
terrifying, occasionally sickening, but you'll definitely want to go
again.

🌍Earth Signs (Taurus, Virgo, Capricorn)
Stable, sensual, dependable.
They're not here for games, or texts that say "wyd?"
Attraction grows through trust and consistency.
Their love language is loyalty,
(and practical gestures like fixing your Wi-Fi).

Dating one feels like: Finally being able to exhale, until they start
rearranging your kitchen "for efficiency."

💨Air Signs (Gemini, Libra, Aquarius) Flirty, cerebral,
unpredictable.
They fall in love with your mind first, then your playlist.
Communication is their kink; boredom is their kryptonite.
Expect late-night debates and occasional ghosting.

Dating one feels like: Starring in your own indie rom-com, clever

Venus, Mars and Vino

dialogue, questionable commitment.

💧Water Signs (Cancer, Scorpio, Pisces)
Deep, intuitive, emotional sponges.
They don't just fall in love; they merge souls.
Passionate, protective, sometimes a little too psychic for comfort.
They crave connection like air (and will drown you in feelings if
you're not ready).
Dating one feels like: Wading into the ocean at night, magical,
mysterious, slightly dangerous, and impossible to forget.

Venus & Mars: The Lovers' Planets

If your sun sign is your personality, your Venus and Mars signs are
your romantic GPS.

Venus = what you want in love.
Mars = how you go after it.

For example:
Venus in Taurus? You want slow, sensual, steady.
Mars in Aries? You chase hard and fast.
Translation: you want candlelit dinners but end up in a chaotic
situation- ships.

When you understand your Venus-Mars combo, your dating
patterns start to make uncomfortable sense, and the rose-tinted
boujee glasses come off!

Compatibility: Cosmic Edition

Let's decode who's most likely to make you swoon and who's most likely to make you block them by the next full moon.

Your Sign	Best Matches	Proceed with Caution	Cosmic Love Note
Aries	Leo, Sagittarius, Gemini	Cancer, Capricorn	You need someone who can keep up, not calm you down.
Taurus	Virgo, Capricorn, Pisces	Leo, Aquarius	You crave loyalty, not theatrics. Pick the doers, not the dreamers.
Gemini	Libra, Aquarius, Aries	Scorpio, Virgo.	Your brain needs foreplay as much as your body. Find someone who keeps up.
Cancer	Scorpio, Pisces, Taurus	Aries, Libra	You love deeply, just don't drown in someone else's tide.
Leo	Aries, Sagittarius, Libra	Taurus, Scorpio	You shine brightest with someone who claps loudest
Scorpio	Cancer, Pisces, Virgo	Gemini, Leo	You attract what you fear, but when you love, it's alchemy.
Sagittarius	Aries, Leo, Aquarius	Virgo, Pisces	You need freedom and fire, never settle for a cage
Capricorn	Taurus, Virgo, Cancer	Aries, Libra	You love through loyalty, not grand gestures.
Aquarius	Gemini, Libra, Sagittarius	Taurus, Scorpio	You need someone who challenges you intellectually, not someone who emotionally drains you.
Pisces	Cancer, Scorpio, Capricorn	Gemini, Sagittarius	You love like a poem.

Venus, Mars and Vino

Star Signs Meet Love Languages

Here's where astrology meets emotional intelligence.

Love Languages and Astrology

Love Language	Who's Likely to Speak It	Cosmic Interpretation
Words of Affirmation	Gemini, Libra, Leo	Communication is foreplay.
Acts of Service	Virgo, Capricorn, Taurus	"I fixed your printer" = "I love you."
Receiving Gifts	Taurus, Leo	It's not about money, it's about *meaning*.
Quality Time	Cancer, Pisces, Scorpio	"I don't want attention, I want presence."
Physical Touch	Aries, Sagittarius	Affection is their default language.

If you can learn your partner's cosmic and emotional dialects, you're basically bilingual in love.

The Danger of "Astro-Excuses"

Let's get this straight: astrology explains behaviour, it doesn't excuse it.

If someone's acting like a walking red flag, don't blame their Mercury retrograde, blame their lack of self-awareness.
"Sorry I ghosted, I'm an Aquarius" is not a personality trait.
Use astrology for insight, not justification. It's a mirror, not a map.

The Cosmic Takeaway

Astrology gives us language for energy, a poetic way to understand attraction, friction, and fate.

It's not about predicting your next relationship; it's about recognising patterns and honouring your own energy.

Whether you're a dreamy Pisces or a fiery Aries, remember: the stars might guide you, but you steer the spacecraft!

Because the most powerful thing you can do with astrology isn't figure out who to love, it's figure out how to love better.

So, we've mapped your star sign, decoded your love language, and probably justified at least one questionable dating decision using Mercury retrograde.

But astrology isn't *just* about compatibility charts and cosmic chemistry; it's also about *energy*.

***

Venus, Mars and Vino

How you show up. How you care. How you connect.
And while we've explored Venus, Mars, and all things sexy and celestial, let's bring that stardust down to Earth right into your daily life.

Because your zodiac energy doesn't switch off when you log out of Hinge or hang up your heels.
It flows into how you eat, move, love, and even how you care for your little four-legged companions.

That's right, the universe didn't stop at your birth chart. It extended the assignment to your pets, too.

Yes, your dog has zodiac drama.
Your cat? Absolutely a Leo.
And your hamster? Probably a Capricorn with control issues.

But here's the bigger picture: learning to understand *their* energy, how they love, trust, and exist in the moment can actually teach *you* more about grounded love than any full moon ritual ever could.

Coming Up Next: Pet Energy & Astrology

Because sometimes the truest lessons about love, patience, and presence come with wagging tails and whiskers, not grand gestures or dating profiles.

"At least my dog gets excited to see me every time and doesn't need to 'check his schedule.'"

🐾✨ Pet Energy & Astrology Mini-Guide

Because your soulmate might actually be your cat.
I guess what I'm possibly getting at here is that if dating isn't working out, just go get yourself a pet!

Astrology doesn't just explain *our* quirks; it totally applies to our four-legged companions, too.
Ever noticed how your dog's dramatic sighs or your cat's mysterious moonlight stares feel suspiciously zodiac-coded?
Let's decode your pet's cosmic personality and what they might be teaching you about love, patience, and snack distribution.

♈ Aries Pets (March 21 – April 19)

Bold, bossy, and always first through the door.
Expect spontaneous zoomies at 3 a.m. and an alarming amount of confidence for someone who still can't spell "sit."

Lesson: *Love can be loud, but it's also fearless.*

♉ Taurus Pets (April 20 – May 20)

The foodie of the zodiac.
Knows exactly when dinner is and won't let you forget it.
Loves naps, cuddles, and soft blankets more than you love Wi-Fi.

Lesson: *Pleasure and routine are self-care, not indulgence.*

♊Gemini Pets (May 21 – June 20)

One minute, they're your best friend, the next, they're staring out the window like they're plotting to join another family.
Social, curious, and occasionally chaotic but never boring.

Lesson: *Keep things playful and stay curious about love.*

♋Cancer Pets (June 21 – July 22)

The emotional support animal of emotional support animals. Loves deep cuddles, home comforts, and staring into your soul.

Lesson: *It's safe to be soft; vulnerability is power.*

♌Leo Pets (July 23 – August 22)

Dramatic, glamorous, and fully aware that they're the stars of your camera roll.
If ignored, will stage a performance worthy of an Oscar.

Lesson: *Know your worth and don't be afraid to demand attention when you deserve it.*

♍ Virgo Pets (August 23 – September 22)

The organised overthinker.
They prefer their toys in a certain spot and may judge your cleaning habits.
Quietly loyal, deeply observant, and the perfect emotional regulator.

Venus, Mars and Vino

Lesson: *Stability and care are the sexiest things alive.*
♎Libra Pets (September 23 – October 22)

Charming, affectionate, and probably gets more likes than you on Instagram.
Can't stand tension in the home, it will distract you mid-argument with an adorable tail wag.

Lesson: *Balance your energy and flirt with life.*

♏Scorpio Pets (October 23 – November 21)

Mysterious, intense, and probably judging you from the shadows. Loyal to their person, but takes time to trust.

Lesson: *Love isn't about control, it's about depth.*

♐Sagittarius Pets (November 22 – December 21)

Adventurous, free-spirited, and occasionally unhinged. If there's mischief to be found, they've already found it.

Lesson: *Never cage joy. Explore. Play. Be wild.*

♑Capricorn Pets (December 22 – January 19)

Old souls in tiny bodies. May have been a CEO in a past life. Takes rules seriously but still appreciates a good belly rub.

Lesson: *Work hard, rest hard, and nap responsibly.*

♒Aquarius Pets (January 20 – February 18)

Eccentric, independent, and low-key, a genius.
Will only cuddle on *their* terms.

Lesson: *Freedom is love's best friend.*

♓Pisces Pets (February 19 – March 20)

Dreamy, gentle, and slightly psychic.
Senses when you're sad and shows up right on cue.

Lesson: *Empathy is your superpower, but protect your energy, too.*

Final Thought:

Your pet's astrology isn't just fun, it's a tiny mirror of your own energy.
They're here to show you what unconditional love looks like…
with a little bit of chaos, fur, and cosmic wisdom sprinkled in.

So next time you're wondering about your love life, maybe ask your dog.
They already know the vibe. 🐕✨

So as we move from **pet energy** to **planetary energy**, remember this: love isn't just grounded; it's also cosmic.
You've mastered the leash, now let's talk about the lunar pull.

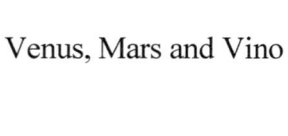

"Super-moon energy: when you're either falling in love or blocking someone at midnight, no in-between."

The Super Moon Effect
Cosmic Chemistry & Celestial Timing

When the Moon Messes with Your Love Life

There's something almost magical about a super-moon, that luminous, oversized orb hanging low and heavy in the night sky, pulling tides, emotions, and text messages you absolutely shouldn't send at 11:47 p.m.

Astrologically, the moon governs emotion, intuition, and the subconscious.
So when it's super, meaning it's closer to Earth than usual, everything feels a little extra.

More feelings.
More nostalgia.
More "maybe I should text my ex just to check they're alive" energy.

Top Tip: DON'T

The Moon as the Mirror of Emotion

In astrology, your moon sign represents your emotional world, how you love, react, and retreat.
It's your inner landscape, the part of you that craves comfort and connection.
***

Venus, Mars and Vino

During a super-moon, that inner world gets amplified.
It's like someone turned your emotional Wi-Fi all the way up. If
you had antennas, they would be flying about like crazy. You feel
everything, deeply, sometimes beautifully, sometimes dramatically.

Think of it as the universe shining a spotlight on whatever needs
release, renewal, or reflection.

So if you're crying over a rom-com, suddenly journaling at 2 a.m.,
or considering a fringe... don't panic.
You're just under celestial influence.

Super-moon Love Energy: The Cosmic Reset

Super-moons often mark moments of revelation or closure in
relationships.
They're emotional checkpoints, endings, beginnings, and big
realisations.
Depending on your zodiac sign, the energy hits differently:

Fire signs (Aries, Leo, Sagittarius): Passion overload.

You're either falling in love or filing emotional restraining orders,
sometimes both in one night.

Earth signs (Taurus, Virgo, Capricorn): You're questioning
commitment and craving stability. Expect major "Is this love or
logistics?" vibes.

Air signs (Gemini, Libra, Aquarius): Communication peaks. You're
either confessing feelings or ghosting mid-sentence.

***

Water signs (Cancer, Scorpio, Pisces): You're emotional, intuitive, and possibly psychic. Romance feels fated, just double-check it's not nostalgia in disguise.

Rituals for Romantic Clarity Under a Super-moon

Because we're not just victims of cosmic chaos, we can harness it.

1. Write it, don't text it.
When emotions run high, journaling saves you from regret.
Write the message you *want* to send, then burn it, not your dignity.

2. Release the old.
Let go of past connections that still linger energetically.
Delete the thread, unfollow the memory, forgive what didn't work.

3. Set new intentions.
Super-moons are powerful portals for manifestation.
Get specific:
"I'm calling in love that feels safe, reciprocal, and aligned." Then step back and let the universe do its thing.

4. Ground yourself.
Touch grass. Literally.
The moon may stir emotion, but your job is to stay anchored in reality.

The Cosmic Connection: Venus, Mars & the Moon

Remember back in the astrology chapter where we explored Venus
and Mars, love and desire?
Well, here's where the moon ties them together.

Venus rules attraction, what (and who) we value. Mars rules action:
how we go after what we want. The Moon rules emotion, and how
safe we feel doing it.

When these three align (especially around a super-moon),
relationships shift. That's why some couples reconnect, others end,
and singles suddenly meet someone who feels destined.

It's not magic, it's energetic timing.

71

Venus, Mars and Vino

The Super-moon & Self-Love

Before you go manifesting soulmates, remember: the moon also represents your inner feminine energy, receptivity, intuition and softness.

The real super-moon magic happens when you turn that energy inward.

Ask yourself:

What do I need emotionally right now?
Am I giving that to myself?
Am I chasing love to fill a void or sharing it from overflow?

The moon reminds us that light waxes and wanes, and so do we.
You're allowed to retreat, reflect, and rest between love stories.

In Summary: Cosmic Love 101

A super-moon doesn't create love; it reveals it.
It highlights what's true, what's ready to end, and what's waiting to begin.

So if your heart feels pulled like the tides, take a breath.
You're not crazy, you're just cosmically in tune.

And when you align your emotional rhythm (Moon), your romantic values (Venus), and your desires (Mars)... that's when love feels less like a storm and more like a symphonic ensemble.

***

Next up
We now leave the lunar lunacy for something far more terrestrial
(and occasionally terrifying):
Men vs Women: The Great Dating Divide.
Because even under the same moon, we're often on different
planets.

"Women Google signs of emotional unavailability; men Google 'why she's mad.'"

Men vs Women: The Great Dating Divide

The Modern Dating Paradox

We live in a time where gender roles are blurring faster than mascara after a breakup, and that's a good thing.

But it also means confusion.
Women want independence and intimacy.
Men want emotional connection but fear vulnerability.
Everyone wants equality until the bill arrives.

The "who texts first" anxiety of the 2000s has evolved into the "who's emotionally available first" crisis of the 2020s.

What Men Actually Want (Not Just Sex)

Let's bust a myth: men aren't just driven by lust. Sure, attraction is visual for many, but emotional safety matters more than they let on.

Men fall for women who make them feel seen, not scrutinised.
They crave admiration as much as affection.
And they love it when someone trusts them to show up, not just perform.

The problem? Many men are taught that vulnerability equals weakness. So instead of saying, "I'm scared of getting hurt," they just… vanish.
Or they turn intimacy into banter to avoid sincerity.

***

Venus, Mars and Vino

If a man jokes too much, it's often his heart trying to whisper through the sarcasm.

What Women Actually Want (Not Just Commitment!)

Women aren't all after marriage and matching pyjamas. They want emotional reciprocity, someone who listens, communicates, and gets it.

They're tired of being therapists in heels.
They don't want to "fix" anyone; they want a partnership, not a project.

Modern women want a man who's emotionally intelligent, self-aware, and confident without being controlling.
Someone who makes space, not noise.

Basically, safe can still be sexy.

Why Communication Fails Between the Sexes

Men and women often speak entirely different emotional dialects.

Men: Process feelings through action. "I'm stressed" = "I'll fix something or go silent."

Women: Process feelings through words. "I'm stressed" = "Please listen while I unpack this entire emotional suitcase."

Men think they're being helpful when they offer solutions. Women think they're being ignored.

***

Women think they're being vulnerable when they share. Men think they're being attacked.

It's not emotional incompatibility; it's emotional loss in translation.

The Gendered Fear Game

Both sexes fear rejection; they just hide it differently.

Men: fear failing Venus, Mars and Vino
Women: fear not being enough.
Top tip- Ladies, you are enough, if you are ever told you're too much, they aren't enough!

He worries he won't measure up. She worries she'll be too much.

So men protect themselves with distance.
Women protect themselves with over-giving.
And both end up exhausted, misunderstood, and halfway through a bottle of wine Googling "how to date like you don't care."

The Ego Tango

Attraction dances with ego more than anyone admits.
Men feel desired when they're chosen. Women feel desired when they're pursued.

But when both wait for the other to make the first move, we get the modern standoff: the double-like on Instagram that goes absolutely nowhere.

We're terrified of rejection, but equally terrified of sincerity.
It's easier to play it cool than to risk being seen.

Venus, Mars and Vino

Masculine & Feminine Energy (Not Gender, Energy)

Forget anatomy, we're talking energy, **not** identity.

Masculine energy: direction, purpose, action.
Feminine energy: creativity, flow, intuition.

Healthy relationships need both partners to be in balance. When both partners lean too far into the same energy, the connection fizzles or clashes.

The dance works when there's polarity, give and receive, push and pull, strength and softness.

You can be a strong, independent woman and still crave being held.
You can be a stoic man and still want to be understood.
Energy isn't gendered, it's relational.

Healed Dating vs Hurt Dating

The difference between dating in your twenties and dating after you've done some therapy, self-discovery or had a whole host of experience….

Boundaries.
Standards.
Emotional literacy.

Hurt dating: "I need someone to fill my void." Healed dating: "I want someone to share my overflow."

Healed people communicate, take accountability, and don't play games.
They don't need to chase; they choose.
They're not looking for rescue, they're looking for resonance.

***

And that's when dating stops being war… and dare I say it, you find peace.

The Funny, Messy Truth

Let's be honest, men and women are both baffling.
Men send mixed signals. Women send novels.
Men panic about commitment.
Women panic about why they panic.
We're all trying to connect, but half the time, we're just decoding each other's trauma responses.

Dating isn't about figuring out the "other side."
It's about understanding your own and meeting someone doing the same.
Venus, Mars and Vino
Because the most attractive thing to any gender, at any age, is emotional maturity wrapped in self-awareness and a hint of humour.
(Making us laugh all the way into the sack!)

Next up: After exploring *Men vs Women* and the ways we connect, misunderstand, and mirror each other, the next chapter begins where the gap between us becomes its sharpest: betrayal.
The Betrayer is not just a person, but a turning point, the moment differences turn into wounds, and expectations crack under the weight of disappointment. But the betrayer's role is significant yet temporary; their purpose is to break the version of you that was too small.
And from that breaking emerges the next evolution of your story.
That is where *Becoming* begins, the chapter where pain becomes power, clarity replaces chaos, and you rise into a version of yourself that could only exist because something, or someone, fell away.

"Disney taught me a lot, mainly that I don't need a prince, but if he arrives, he'd better come with emotional intelligence and a fully charged phone."

From Betrayal To Becoming: The Healed Dating Era

Welcome to Healed Dating

Welcome to the era where romance gets rewritten by you.

This isn't about finding *the one.*
It's about becoming the woman who knows she already is.

Healed dating starts when attraction aligns with your energy, not your ego.
When connection matters more than chemistry. When you flirt with life itself before you flirt with anyone else.

It's love, but with boundaries, balance, and better taste in wine.

The Healing Hangover

After heartbreak, everyone swears they're "taking time for themselves."
Translation: crying to Adele, overanalysing red flags, and googling *"is emotional detachment spiritual growth?"*

Healing isn't linear; it's a messy cocktail of peace and panic.
One minute you're journaling affirmations, the next you're deep-stalking their new girlfriend's Etsy shop.

The real work isn't rushing back into love; it's sitting with the silence long enough to hear your own voice again.

Healed Dating: The Grown-Up Glow-Up

Healed dating is like upgrading from boxed wine to a vintage bottle, smoother, wiser, far less headache-inducing.

It looks like this:
- You don't chase. You attract.
- You ask direct questions instead of decoding emojis.
- You're turned on by emotional availability (wild, I know).
- You can say "this isn't for me" without drafting a TED Talk about boundaries.

It's when you stop auditioning for love and start interviewing for partnership.

Stop-Gap Love: The Rebound That Teaches

Then there's the *stopgap*, that fun, sexy, mildly chaotic in-between. They're not "the one," but they remind you you're still alive.

They reignite your spark, show you your progress, and maybe confirm you still have a type (and still need to retire it).

Just don't confuse a *lesson* for a *lifetime.*
Love them for what they were, a bridge back to yourself, and move forward with grace (and great hair).

The Plaster-Ripped-Off Era

(Ah... The wholesome whore stage)
Ah, yes, the glorious, slightly unhinged chapter where you
remember you're hot, free, and feral in the best way.
You flirt, you laugh, you rediscover your power.
You date for the story, not the security.
You collect experiences instead of red flags.
It's not about being reckless, it's about being *reclaimed.*
You're not running from pain; you're running toward pleasure,
autonomy, and your own aliveness.
Casual can be healing, if you're honest.
Don't sell "detached" when you secretly crave devotion.
Honesty with yourself is the real flex.

The Self-Worth Filter

This is where everything changes.
You stop mistaking attention for affection.
You stop calling inconsistency "chemistry."
You realise peace isn't boring, it's rare.

Your new lens looks like this:

- Do they add calm or chaos?
- Do they communicate or confuse?
- Do I feel seen or sized up?

If they don't meet the standard, it's *"thank you, next"* with
gratitude, not bitterness.

Because healed love doesn't chase closure, it

chooses clarity.

"Betrayal: The Plot Twist Nobody Ordered"

We all have one heartbreak story that makes our friends pause
mid–Prosecco sip and say, "Babe… WHAT?"
Mine came with the kind of twist that knocks the wind out of you,
not because of who I lost, but because of who I found myself
becoming in the aftermath.

When I discovered my ex had been giving parts of himself away in
places trust should never have to stretch, it felt like my world
cracked.
Not just from the betrayal itself, but from the realisation that the
relationship I thought I was in… wasn't the one he was living.

There's a special kind of pain in loving someone who treats loyalty
like an optional extra, a "nice to have" instead of a non-negotiable.
At first, I asked myself the classic hits:
*Was I not enough? Did I miss the signs? Was I foolish for believing in
us?*
But healing brought clarity, and clarity brought truth:
His actions were never a reflection of my worth, only a reflection
of his wounds.

People who don't know how to sit with their discomfort will
always look for escape routes and excuses.

People who can't hold depth will always look for distraction.
People who fear intimacy will always sabotage the closest thing to
a real connection they've ever had.

But here's the part that saved me:

Cheating doesn't expose your flaws; it exposes their limits.

I stopped replaying the "why" and started focusing on the "what now."
And *what now* looks like choosing self-respect over self-doubt.

It looks like understanding that closure doesn't always come packaged with an apology.
Sometimes closure is simply peace, the peace of knowing you didn't betray yourself.

Betrayal hurts, but it also reveals.
It shows you what you will never tolerate again.
It hands you back to yourself.
It becomes the moment you stop being the supporting character in someone else's chaos and become the author of your own healing.

You didn't lose someone who valued you.
You lost someone who didn't know how to.

And that's not your heartbreak, that's your liberation.

Reflection: From Red Flags to Realignment

What lesson lived underneath the betrayal?
How can I show myself the loyalty I kept giving away?
Where do I still confuse drama with depth?
What does integrity look like for me, and how will I recognise it next time?

Dating After Healing: The Soft Start

When you truly heal, dating becomes less of a performance and more of a conversation.

You stop strategising.
You stop pretending.
You show up as yourself, awkward, hopeful, whole.
You no longer search for someone to love you *right*; you invite someone who fits into the love you've already built for yourself.

That's the real glow-up: love that's calm, conscious, and completely aligned.

The 3-Phase Love Timeline

1.**Breakdown**: You lose yourself in love.
2.**Breakthrough**: You find yourself again.
3.**Break Free**: You date with discernment, not desperation.

Every heartbreak is a curriculum.

Each chapter of your life is an entertaining page turner.
Healed dating?
That's your graduation.

Now for a little fun.....

And this came to me whilst I watched Disney Plus whilst writing this book (as you do)

Let us just take all of this in and think about the New Age Princess era.

The Rise of the independent Princess (Yep, that's you)

Moana' Energy • Pocahontas' Standards • Belle's Boundaries

Once upon a time, princesses sat in castles waiting for a man with
a sword, a horse, and questionable breath control to rescue them.
Now?
We've evolved.

We're in the era of **Independent Princesses**, women who don't
need saving, but will happily accept a latte.

Because let's be honest:

**Moana didn't wait for a prince; she literally got in a boat,
fought a lava demon, and fixed the world.**
That's the energy we're bringing to dating now.

**Pocahontas wasn't swooning over bare-minimum behavior, she
sang to trees, talked to spirits, and told a man with a bowl-cut
to sit down and listen.**
That's boundaries AND communication, babe.

**Belle didn't take any shit from the Beast; she refused dinner,
demanded respect, and made him earn her softness.**
That's healed dating, right there.

These women redefined what it means to be feminine, powerful,
and emotionally intelligent, all at once.
And we're finally catching up.

Venus, Mars and Vino

What the Modern Princess Era Actually Means

1.You rescue yourself first.
The right partner joins your story; they don't rewrite your script.

2.You don't "fix" the Beast.
He either grows…
or he stays in the castle with the broken furniture.

3.You don't chase potential.
We're not collecting projects, we're building partnerships.

4.You're soft AND strong.
Moana cried.
Belle read books.
Pocahontas meditated.
Strength isn't hardness; it's knowing your worth.

5.You choose love, not survival.
And that's why the love you choose now will be better than any before.

Gaston (Beauty and the Beast): The Blueprint for Modern Red-Flag Masculinity

Why does the modern princess era exist in the first place?

Every generation has *that* man, the charming one, the confident one, the one who's absolutely convinced he's God's gift to women and protein powder.
I had one I dated that had the audacity to call me vain and attention seeking, whilst his own Instagram grid was simply images of his own 'inner Gaston!'

***

I guess we are all entitled to our own opinions, you do you, honey.

Disney gave us the early prototype: **Gaston.**

And honestly?
He's still alive and well, just with better haircuts and worse Instagram habits.

Let's break him down.
The Modern Gaston Checklist

If you've dated in the last decade, you've met at least one.

Overconfidence posing as charisma

Gaston walks into a room as if he owns it.
Modern Gaston walks into a bar, gym, or Hinge profile like it's a runway designed just for him.
You must have seen the professional photo shoot bios. (Ick)

Confidence is sexy.
Arrogance? Not so much.

Obsessed with aesthetics

Gaston: "No one's slick as Gaston…"
Modern version: gym mirror selfies, flexing pics, "5'8 but 6'2 in vibes."

He wants admiration, not connection.

Venus, Mars and Vino

Thinks persistence = romance

Gaston ignored Belle's boundaries.
Modern Gaston double-texts, triple-DMs, and
sends a voice note if you don't reply in 12 minutes.

"No" is just another challenge to him.

Wants the beauty but not the brains

He doesn't want an equal.
He wants an accessory.

He wants Belle's face, not Belle's spine.

Modern Gaston?
He'll say things like:

- "You're too independent."
- "You're intimidating."
- "I miss the old you." (Translation: the version he could control.)

Collects validation like trophies

Gaston needed a crowd cheering him on.
Modern Gaston needs:

- likes
- followers
- female attention
- constant praise
- a rotating supply of matches for "ego maintenance"
It's not love he craves; it's audience engagement.

Lacks emotional depth

Feelings? Gaston doesn't know her.
Vulnerability? Blocked.
Therapy? Absolutely not, unless it's couples
therapy he's dragged into.

Modern Gaston calls anything deeper than surface-level affection
"too much drama."

Projects insecurity as dominance

The loudest guy in the room is often the one most terrified of real
intimacy.
Gaston isn't strong.
He's scared.
And modern Gaston hides fear with bravado, control, and inflated
masculinity.

***

👑Why Modern Princesses Don't Entertain Gaston Anymore

Because Belle walked away…
and so will we.

Modern princesses are:

- Independent
- Self-aware
- Trauma-informed
- Therapy-friendly
- Emotionally literate
- Done raising someone else's grown son

We're the Moanas, the Belles, the Pocahontases:

Women who choose freedom, wisdom, softness,
boundaries, and alignment.

We don't swoon at a man's biceps.
We swoon at a man's consistency.

We don't want a protector who intimidates us,
we want a partner who respects us.
We want a man who can communicate, not just lift
heavy things.

💬 Gaston in the Dating World Today

You'll find him:

- Flexing in a gym selfie
- Performing masculinity
- Bragging without substance
- Chasing admiration
- Fearing emotional depth
- Mislabelling confidence as entitlement
- Misinterpreting boundaries as rejection

He's not a villain.
He's just unevolved.

But modern women?
We've evolved.

And now Gaston is not a threat,
he's a cautionary tale in tight trousers.

The Takeaway

In short, the Gastons still exist.
They are alive, flexing, and sending "wyd?" at
11:47 pm.

But here's the real takeaway:

***

Modern princesses don't fight for Gaston.
We outgrow him.
We outwalk him.
We outglow him.

And sometimes?
We out-move him, literally.

Because once you stop entertaining men who need applause more than accountability, you naturally step into your next era…
The era where you pack your metaphorical (or literal) bags, choose yourself, and rewrite the script.

Which brings me neatly to The Holiday.
Yes, *that* Holiday.
The film, in which Cameron Diaz has had enough, slams a door with perfect eyeliner, and reinvents her entire life in one dramatic location change.

And honestly?

I've lived that storyline.
Just with slightly less snow… and definitely less Jude Law.

The Holiday Era: Channelling Your Inner Cameron Diaz

If the Independent Princess Era had a film adaptation, it would absolutely be *The Holiday,* but specifically the Cameron Diaz storyline, because let's be honest… Kate Winslet gives cottage core healing, while Cameron gives chaotic, glamorous reinvention energy.

***

Venus, Mars and Vino

And I?
I have always felt more Cameron.

She moves countries on impulse.
She throws herself into new beginnings with a suitcase full of
denial and lip gloss.
She doesn't cry until she really, REALLY does.
She's successful, confident, emotionally competent in work…
and an absolute hot mess in love.

Sound familiar?

Because here's the plot twist:
I also moved to a new town, a quiet country spot just outside
London, for a man.
A man who turned out to be less "Jude Law in a knitted jumper"
and more "seasonal disappointment with delusions of grandeur."

It went wrong.
Hellishly wrong.
The kind of wrong that makes you stare out of a frosty window
like you're in an Adele music video.
But here's where the Cameron Diaz energy kicks in:

She didn't pack up her life and fly across the world for a man.
She did it for herself.
The man was the excuse, the transformation was the point.

That's the real magic of this era:

✨ You get to start over somewhere new.
✨ You get to reinvent yourself without needing

permission.

✨ You get to rediscover your peace in a place where nobody knows your heartbreak history.
You don't need a snow-covered cottage or a widowed book editor single dad to validate your fresh start.
(But if one appears, I won't stop you.)

You just need the courage to rewrite your story, loudly, sassily, unapologetically, the way Cameron Diaz slams that iconic wooden door and declares she's DONE being mistreated.

And as much as I admire Belle, Moana, and Pocahontas…

Cameron Diaz was my modern princess moment: the woman who left, broke down, rebuilt, and found herself somewhere entirely unexpected.
Because sometimes the fairytale isn't falling in love.
Sometimes the fairytale is leaving.

From Healing to Swiping

So here's the thing, you've done the work, princess…

You've cried, journaled, detoxed, blocked, healed, and glowed.

You've reclaimed your peace, your playlist, and your power.

Now comes the part where you take that healed heart back out into the world, not to prove anything, but to play again.

(Ding Ding, Round 2!)
***

Venus, Mars and Vino

Because love, when you're healed, hits differently.
It's not about filling a void anymore; it's about expanding your joy.

So, as you re-enter the dating scene, whether it's through pixels, playlists, or a chance encounter in Lidl's middle aisle, remember:

You're not auditioning; you're curating.
You're not searching; you're selecting.

You're not hoping for love to find you; you're ready for it to meet you where you already are grounded, glowing, and gloriously unbothered.

STOP looking for the Love of your life!

(Top Tip, That's you, you god damn, sexy, son of a bitch!)

Now, let's talk dating apps, the modern jungle gym of love, lust, and logistics.

Grab your phone, your standards, and your sense of humour.

Let's find you a man you can trust with your Thursday night tanning ritual, who has your back (literally)

Coming up next....Welcome to the shit show:

Digital Dating, Bios, Profiles & the Online vs Organic Dilemma.

Where we tackle the algorithmic jungle of modern romance, teaching you how to flirt like a pro online, write a killer bio, and spot love-bombers with your eyes closed.

But first, a little fun!

QUIZ: Which Independent Princess Energy Are You?

Circle what feels most like you, no judgment, no singing animals required.

1. Your love language looks like...

A. Adventure, challenge, spontaneity (Moana)
B. Depth, intuition, emotional courage (Pocahontas)
C. Conversation, curiosity, "teach me something" (Belle)

2. On a date, you value...

A. Someone who keeps up with your vision Venus, Mars and Vino
B. Someone aligned with your morals and energy
C. Someone who stimulates your mind

3. Your biggest dating ick is...

A. Laziness or lack of ambition
B. Closed-mindedness
C. Poor communication skills

4. Your healing era looks like...

A. Booking flights and rediscovering yourself
B. Grounding, journaling, nature walks
C. Therapy, self-reflection, reading relationship books (like this one)

5. Your greatest strength in love is...

A. Bravery
B. Compassion
C. Wisdom

***

Your Princess Energy Results

Mostly A — Moana Energy

You don't wait to be chosen — you choose the direction. You're brave, intuitive, and allergic to stagnation. You need a partner who fuels your fire, not dims it.

Mostly B — Pocahontas Energy

You love with depth and intuition.
You're a peaceful warrior: grounded, empathetic, and spiritually plugged-in.
You need a partner who respects your values and protects your peace.

Mostly C — Belle Energy

You want emotional intelligence, conversation, and growth. You'll walk away from any Beast who refuses to evolve.
You need a partner who meets you at your level — intellectually and emotionally.

The Independent Princess Era Manifesto
Soft heart. Strong boundaries. Zero delusion.

Thou shalt remember…..

I am not waiting in a tower.
If I want something, I climb down, grab my bag, and go get it myself.
I do not chase potential.
I choose partnership, not projects.

I am soft because I am strong.
My gentleness is not a weakness; it is a superpower.

I am not here to fix the Beast.
If he wants my heart, he must meet me where I am, not where he left his last excuse.

I don't lose my voice for love.
I speak my needs, my truth, my worth, clearly and unapologetically.

I don't confuse chaos with passion.
Peace is my new form of chemistry.
Consistency is my new love language.

I don't shrink from being chosen.
I expand, and anyone meant for me expands with me.

I am not for everyone, and that is my magic.
The right person won't be intimidated by my power or my softness.

I honour my inner child, my present self, and my future woman.

Venus, Mars and Vino

All three deserve the healthiest, happiest version of love.

I don't fear walking away.
I fear wasting my time on anything that dims my glow.

I choose myself every day.
And anyone who walks beside me must choose themselves too.

* * *

I am the writer of my own story.
The heroine.
The healer.
The plot twist.
The happy ending.

This is my Independent Princess Era, and
I am the one I've been waiting for.

"Dating is like pushing your tray along in a cafeteria: nothing looks good, but you know you have to pick something by the time you get to the cashier."

Marsha Warfield.

Digital Dating: Bios, Profiles & the Online vs Organic Dilemma

Chapter 11: Digital Dating, Bios, Profiles & the Online vs Organic Dilemma

Congratulations, darling, you're officially healed, hydrated, and emotionally available.

Now comes the next frontier: finding love (or at least a decent coffee date) in the wild, algorithmic jungle we call modern dating.

Let's be honest, online dating is both a blessing and a battlefield. It's like ordering takeaway for your heart: convenient, full of options, but occasionally disappointing when it arrives looking nothing like the photos.

But here's the twist: this time, you're not swiping from loneliness. You're swiping from *strength.*

You're not looking for someone to complete you; you're seeing who can complement you.

Because healed dating energy hits different, you can spot a red flag through a well-lit selfie.
You can tell the difference between "mysterious" and "emotionally unavailable."
And you know what's sexier than abs or astrology? Effort.

The Modern Dating Landscape

Once upon a time, love stories began in bookshops, coffee queues, or shared taxis in the rain.

Now they begin with "You up?" and end with "seen 11:03 p.m."

But that's okay, because this time, you're the main character *and* the narrator. (Why do I hear Morgan Freeman's voice when I'm writing this!)

You'll navigate it all with style, humour, and the kind of self-respect that even bad Wi-Fi can't mess with.

In this chapter, we'll cover:
-How to write a bio that feels like *you*, not your CV.
-Choosing photos that say "emotionally available, but fun."
-The fine art of first messages (For the record, it's not "hey").
-When to trust your gut, and when to hit "un match."
Because you're not just dating anymore, you're curating *alignment*, not attention.

The Matador Moment

My friend once told me I dated like a matador, sprinting straight toward the red flags, waving my optimism like a cape.
And honestly?
They weren't wrong.

There was something intoxicating about the chase, the drama, the chemistry, the "maybe this time it's different."
It usually wasn't.
***

But that's the beauty of healed dating: you learn that peace is a
bigger thrill than chaos.
You retire the cape, keep the confidence, and realise the real flex is
not chasing what's waving danger in your face.

Now, instead of charging at red flags, I simply step aside… and let
them run right past me.

A Reality Check Before You Swipe

Not everyone online is emotionally fluent; some are still speaking in
hieroglyphics.
You'll meet the ghosters, the love-bombers, the zombies, the "I'm
not looking for anything serious" philosophers.
On dating apps, I can safely say I Google-searched many
descriptive terms people used, sometimes with wine for
entertainment, and yes, I extended my vocabulary and laughed out
loud, A LOT.

But here's the beauty of healed dating:
You no longer make their behaviour mean something about *you.*

You don't spiral, you swipe on.
You don't chase, you choose.
And you don't lose your sense of humour, because laughter, darling,
is the best filter of all.

More wrinkle-inducing muscles are used when we are sad, so smile
wide, sweety.

Online vs Organic: The Modern Love Debate

Let's be real, online dating gets a bad reputation, but so does waiting for fate in a coffee shop.

Online dating: efficient, diverse, mildly addictive.
You can meet someone in another postcode before your latte cools.
Organic dating: romantic, spontaneous… and about as rare as someone reading this in paperback on public transport.

The truth? Both have their charm and their pitfalls.
Online love starts with *data*. Organic love starts with *dopamine*.
The goal? Blend both: authenticity meets opportunity.

Creating Your Dating Profile: The Digital Shop Window

Your profile isn't a curriculum vitae, it's a *vibe*.
Think: genuine, confident, playful, not "LinkedIn but flirty."

Photos:

- No group shots (no one wants to play *Where's Wally?* with your friends).
- One smiling, one candid, one full-length, one doing something you love.
- Ditch the car selfies. And the sunglasses. You're not in witness protection.

Bio:
- Avoid clichés like "Love to laugh, "partner in crime," or "fluent in sarcasm."
- Tell a story. Be specific. "True crime podcast addict who still cries at Pixar films" > "Netflix and chill."
- Be funny, not mean. Snark isn't sexy.

Venus, Mars and Vino

Prompts:
Answer like you're chatting, not auditioning.

"The way to my heart is…" "Remembering my coffee order and using a real profile picture."
"A green flag I look for…" "Emotional availability and consistent texting. Groundbreaking, I know."

Writing a Bio That Actually Works

Think of your bio as your energy distilled into three sentences.

Formula:
1 line about you
+ 1 line about what you love
+ 1 line about what you're looking for (with a wink).

Example:

"Bookworm, brunch enthusiast, and recovering people-pleaser. Love languages: coffee refills and honesty.
Looking for someone who can handle sarcasm and silence in equal measure."

It's flirty, grounded, and says: *I know who I am.*

* * *

How to Introduce Yourself (Without Cringing)

"Hey" is the beige paint of greetings.

Start strong:

- Comment on something specific in their profile.
- Ask a fun, open-ended question ("Your dog looks like a legend, what's his name?").
- Add humour: "You seem like someone who'd steal all the blankets. I respect that level of confidence."

Flirting online is *tone management*, playful, not performative; warm, not weird.

The Online Archetypes (and How to Handle Them)

Welcome to the cast of characters you'll inevitably meet:

1. **The Ghoster** - Vanishes mid-conversation. Blame bad Wi-Fi (and worse communication skills).
2. **The Zombie** -Resurfaces months later with "Hey stranger." Delete. Again.
3. **The Love Bomber** -Intense early energy, zero follow-through. Big words, small bandwidth.
4. **The Codependent** - Falls for your potential, not your present.
5. **The Grounded One** -Emotionally intelligent, communicative, probably into therapy. Keep them.

Each one teaches you something -even if it's just better boundaries.

* * *

Venus, Mars and Vino

►Online Red Flags to Swipe Left On

►No bio -effort level: zero.
►All group photos -possible witness protection.
►"Looking for fun, nothing serious" -translation: emotional
unavailability dressed as honesty.
►"Drama-free"- ironically, a magnet for drama.
►"Just ask" -no thanks, we're not playing 20 Questions.

Once upon a time, I'd have charged straight toward these -my inner
matador ready for battle, cape in hand.
Now? I simply smile, sip my coffee, and swipe left with peace in
my heart and mascara still perfectly intact.

Because the real glow-up isn't avoiding red flags- it's recognising
them and choosing not to dance.

The Algorithm Isn't the Enemy

Dating apps aren't evil; they're just mirrors.
They reflect your energy, your effort, and your intentions.

Don't treat them like slot machines of self-worth.
Don't chase matches for validation.
And never let rejection rewrite your confidence, sometimes it's just
the algorithm deciding you're out of range.

Your worth isn't measured by matches. It's measured by *alignment*.

* * *

From Online to Offline: First Date Flow

You've matched, the banter's flowing, the vibe is good. Now what?

Golden Rules

- Meet somewhere public (coffee, daylight, not his flat "for a movie").
- Always have your own transport.
- End the date when it peaks, not when it drags.
- Chemistry is a bonus, not a requirement.

Not every date has to be *the one*; sometimes it's just practice for the right one.

Listen to Friends & Family (But Trust Yourself More)

Your friends mean well, but they're not in your relationship. Listen to their red-flag radar, but trust your own gut.

And when family ask, "When are you settling down?" just smile and say, "When it's worth it."

You're not behind, you're becoming.

Claire's Law: Dating Safely in the Modern World

(Because intuition is great, but information is power.)

Let's talk safety, the unsexy but essential side of dating that nobody puts on their profile.

You've done the healing, the glow-up, the boundaries, the bios…

Now let's make sure you also have the **right information** when you need it.

Enter: **Claire's Law**, officially known as *The Domestic Violence Disclosure Scheme* in the UK.

It exists for one powerful reason:
To give you the right to know if someone you're dating has a history of violent or abusive behaviour.

This isn't about paranoia.
It's about protection.
It's about saying:
"My safety matters as much as my love life."

It possibly saved my life this year and a whole host of issues. Every single/dating female should utilise this and thank goodness it exists.

What Claire's Law Actually Allows You to Do

You can formally request information from the police if you're concerned about someone you're dating, or someone a friend or relative is dating.

There are two parts:

The "Right to Ask"

If you're worried about someone's behaviour, controlling, aggressive, inconsistent, or manipulative, you can apply to find out if they have a violent or abusive past.

***

112

No drama.
No judgment.
Just information so you can make an informed decision.

The "Right to Know"

If the police believe you're at risk, they can *proactively* tell you,
even if you never asked.

Why It Matters (Especially in Modern Dating)

Online dating has made it easier than ever to meet wonderful
people. But it has also made it easier for dangerous people to hide
in plain sight.

Red flags are useful.
Gut feelings are powerful.
But **facts** are undeniable.

Claire's Law is not a guarantee that someone is safe, but it's a vital
tool in your toolkit.

Because you're not just dating for chemistry anymore.
You're dating for safety, peace, and longevity.

How to Use Claire's Law
(Practical, Not Panic-Inducing)

If something feels *off*, even slightly:
Sudden rage,
Controlling behaviour,
Scary jealousy,
Love-bombing followed by coldness,

Venus, Mars and Vino

***

Obsessive monitoring,
Financial control,
Explosive reactions to small things
…you're allowed to check.
It's private and confidential.
You won't be judged. You won't get in trouble.
You don't have to be in a relationship to ask, even early dating counts.

You only get one life.
What you do with that life matters.

A Modern Woman's Reminder

Checking someone's past doesn't mean you're paranoid.
It means you've stopped ignoring your intuition.
It means you've learned from past hurt.
It means you value yourself.

And honestly?

A healed woman doesn't just choose better
She protects herself better.

Add This to Your Dating Toolkit:
Trust your gut.
Listen to friends.
Keep your standards.
And if needed…

***

Use Claire's Law.

Because real love should feel safe.
Not scary.
Not confusing. Not
chaotic.

Safe.

Personal Reflection:
When I Learned that **Safety Isn't Overreacting**

I used to think that asking questions, double-checking details, or
trusting my gut made me "dramatic."
I worried I'd look paranoid… or like I didn't trust people enough…
or like I wasn't "chill" enough.

But looking back?
The moments I ignored my instincts were the moments I paid for
later. It took me a long time and a few heartbreaks to understand
this truth:

Wanting to feel safe is not overreacting.
It's self-respect.

If past-me had known about Claire's Law, she might have walked
away sooner.
She might've trusted the discomfort in her stomach instead of the
excuses she was given.
She might've saved herself a lot of emotional bruises, confusion,
and late-night overthinking.

But present-me?
I know better.
***

Venus, Mars and Vino

I know that safety isn't a luxury; it's the foundation. I know that
peace is a green flag, not a boring one.
I know that love should never feel like a gamble with my well-
being.

So now, if something feels off, I check.
If something feels wrong, I step back.
And if something feels unsafe, I walk away, quickly and without
apology.

Because healed women don't just choose better partners.
We choose better protection.
We choose better boundaries.
We choose ourselves.

And if using a law created to protect women makes me "too
cautious," then I'm proud to be cautious
and alive,
and informed,
and safe.
"If peace isn't present, neither am I."

The Sweet Spot: Online Meets Organic

The healthiest love stories begin with one thing: *openness.*

Be open to meeting someone anywhere, online, at the gym, at the
supermarket, even in traffic.
Because the real magic isn't where you meet, it's *how you show up.*

Show up healed. Show up honestly. Show up hopeful.

When you do, the algorithm of the universe works just as well as
Hinge!

Closing Thought

Dating after healing isn't about finding perfection; it's about finding peace. It's about showing up with humour, honesty, and heart, knowing that you no longer need chaos to feel chemistry.

I used to run toward red flags, my inner matador chasing intensity, thinking it was passion.

Now, I raise my own: the ones that say, *"I know my worth, I honour my peace, and I'm no longer available for lessons I've already learned."*

Because the goal isn't to win the game, it's to change how you play it. And when you lead with self-respect, the right people won't make you chase; they'll meet you where you stand.

Once you stop chasing red flags, something magical happens: you start noticing the green ones.
The calm messages. The consistent energy. The people who don't confuse you for content.

And as you re-enter the modern dating arena, wiser, funnier, and a little more fluent in self-respect, it helps to know the language.

Welcome to: **The Modern Dating Dictionary**, your guide to decoding the wild, wonderful, and occasionally ridiculous vocabulary of love in the digital age.

We'll decode today's love lingo, from ghosting to bread crumbing and teach you how to keep your humour (and your heart) intact in a world full of mixed signals.

"I miss old-school romance, like someone calling your house phone and speaking to your mum."

The Modern Dating Dictionary

Because if you're going to date in the digital era, you need to try to speak the language.

Welcome to the linguistic jungle of modern love, where half the words didn't exist ten years ago, and the other half shouldn't exist now.

Consider this your essential phrasebook for navigating romance, red flags, and relationship roulette with your sanity (and SPF) intact.

Ghosting

When someone disappears like they've been raptured, except they're still posting on Instagram two minutes later.
Translation: Emotionally unavailable. Poor communication. Zero courage.

Zombie-ing

When a ghost suddenly rises from the dead and messages you with "Hey stranger," as if they didn't vanish like mist.
Translation: They're bored. You're a convenience, not a priority.

Love Bombing

When someone gives you intense affection, big words, future plans, and soulmate-level energy… Then it fades, soon to pop back up after a disagreement!
Translation: It's not love, it's emotional fireworks with no fire safety plan.

Bread crumbing

Leaving tiny crumbs of attention, just enough to keep you around, never enough to move forward.
Translation: A situation ship with scenic views and no destination.

Benching

Keeping someone "warm" for later, like emotional meal prep.
Translation: You're plan B… or C… or D.

Slow Fading

Instead of ghosting, they fade out gradually, less texting, fewer plans, dwindling enthusiasm.
Translation: Cowardice with a polite mask.

Orbiting

They don't talk to you… but they watch every story you post like you're their personal Netflix series.
Translation: They like access, not commitment.

Soft Launching

Posting a drink across the table… a mystery shoulder… a silhouette.
Translation: "I'm dating someone, but I want to keep my options open."

Situationship

A relationship with all the behaviours of dating, minus clarity, titles, intention, and respect.
Translation: Confusion with benefits.

Thirst Trapping

Posting a sexy photo for attention, validation, or to remind someone you're still extremely hot.
Translation: Strategic ego maintenance.

The Ick

The sudden, irreversible ickiness that turns attraction into pure repulsion after one tiny thing they do.
Translation: Your intuition is throwing a tantrum, and it's usually right.

Future Faking

Making big, dreamy promises about holidays, houses, or babies… with no actual intention to follow through.
Translation: Verbal glitter. Zero substance.

Masking

When someone gives you their "best self" at the start to impress you, then slowly reveals their true personality.
Translation: The demo version expires in month two.

Red Flag Recycling

Dating the same person in a different body because you haven't updated your subconscious "type" yet.
Translation: Trauma picking your partners for you.

***

Venus, Mars and Vino

Dry Dating

Sober dates, clarity without cocktails.
Translation: Brave. Honest. Grown-up.
Can look like- "Coffee and a walk?"
Be careful with this one, as we already touched on being in a public place for the first few, remember?

The Soft No

"I'm just really busy right now." "Not looking for anything serious." "I'm terrible at texting."
Translation: They're rejecting you, without having to say it out loud.

Main Character Energy

Showing up as the star of your own life, not the understudy in someone else's.
Translation: Healed. Glowing. Unbothered.

Green Flag

Therapy, consistency, clear communication, emotional maturity, kindness, and accountability.
Translation: Sexy. Rare. Keep them.

And finally... **The Hard Boundary**

When you recognise your worth, enforce your standards, and stop tolerating situations that drain you.
Translation: Healing unlocked. Welcome to your new era.

***

Modern dating teaches you one thing: your self-care routine needs to be stronger than their mixed signals.

You've done the heart work, now let's honour the outer glow too. In this last chapter, I'll share the self-care and skin rituals that protect your peace as powerfully as your SPF protects your skin.

"You can't control the apps, the algorithm, or the Aries, but you can control your moisturiser."

"Some people age you faster than the sun; that's why emotional SPF matters."

Skin & Self-Care: SPF vs Red Flags

SPF vs Red Flags

Let's get something straight: both sun damage and toxic relationships are sneaky, gradual, and show up years later if you don't protect yourself early.

You can't always see the harm straight away, but it's there, quietly doing its thing beneath the surface.

SPF = Boundaries.

You put it on before exposure. You reapply when things get intense. And you don't skip it just because it's cloudy and "he seems nice."

Because the healed princess, charm has UVA energy, it penetrates deep

The Glow-Up Philosophy

Self-care isn't about bubble baths and candles (though we love those).
It's about building daily habits that whisper:
"I've got me."

Here's how to protect your emotional and physical glow:

1. Morning Rituals:
Wake up early, before the world does and use that time for you!
Start with hydration, SPF, and gratitude, a three-step system for your skin, soul, and sanity.

Throw in a shot of anti-inflammatory turmeric and some multivitamins for good measure.

2.Emotional Cleansing:
Just like exfoliation, let go of what's dulling your shine, old grudges, outdated beliefs, or exes who still view your stories "by accident."
3.Consistency > Intensity:
Whether it's skincare or healing, small daily actions beat dramatic one-time fixes.
4.Rest is Productive:
Your skin and nervous system both need recovery time. You can't glow if you're constantly in fight-or-flight (or fight-with-your-partner) mode.

The "Skin Barrier" Metaphor: Boundaries, Baby

Your skin barrier keeps the good stuff in and the bad stuff out. Your emotional boundaries do the same.

If you over-exfoliate (overgive), overexpose (overshare), or neglect to protect yourself (no boundaries), you end up raw and vulnerable.

Protect your peace like you'd protect your skin's barrier: gently, consistently, and without apology.

And when someone doesn't respect your boundaries? That's not "sensitive skin," that's a red flag rash.

***

Red Flags to Avoid (for Skin and Soul)

Love Bombing = Harsh Exfoliant. Feels amazing at first, then burns later.
Ghosting = Emotional Blackheads. You think they're gone, but they always pop back up.
Mixed Signals = Fragrance Overload. Smells nice, but gives you a headache.
Codependency = Clogged Pores. No space to breathe or grow.
Neglect = No Moisturiser. You dry up emotionally and physically.
Protect your glow. Choose soothing over stimulating.

The Self-Care Spectrum

There's a difference between escape care and sacred care.

- **Escape care:** binge-watching, shopping sprees, postbreakup haircuts. Fun, fleeting, fine in moderation.
- **Sacred care:** journaling, therapy, saying no, moving your body, drinking water, therapy (yes, twice).

The goal isn't perfection, it's presence.
You don't have to "fix" yourself to be worthy of love. You just have to treat yourself like someone worth looking after.

Your Inner Glow Routine

Let's make it official: your glow-up is now a lifestyle.

Cleanse – Let go of what's no longer serving you.
Tone – Reconnect w99ith your boundaries.
Moisturise – Nourish your body, mind, and energy.
SPF – Protect your peace. Always.

Venus, Mars and Vino

Love is optional. Self-care is non-negotiable.
In Summary: The Real Glow-Up

You can buy serums, but you can't fake self-respect.
You can chase validation, but you'll still crave inner calm.

The secret to radiance in skin and soul is maintenance through mindfulness.

Because the real glow-up isn't changing your face or your status, it's falling in love with your own reflection and never dimming your shine for anyone who doesn't deserve the light.

And there it is, your bespoke lesson in love, light, and a really solid skincare routine.

Because when you strip away the dating apps, the astrology charts, and the endless "what are we?" conversations, you're left with the one relationship that truly defines everything else: the one you have with yourself.

You've learned to spot red flags, not romanticise them.
You've learned that healing isn't a phase, it's a lifelong flex.
And you've learned that the glow-up isn't about getting someone's attention; it's about remembering you were radiant all along.

So here's your happily ever after: a life where you choose love that adds peace, SPF that saves face, and boundaries that protect both.

Because the real end game isn't finding "the one," it's being the one. The one who's healed, whole, and still shining, with flawless skin, fierce energy, and zero tolerance for emotional UV damage.

***

Now go out there and live it, glowing, grounded, and gloriously untouchable.

SPF on.
Standards high.
Heart open.

They say beauty is only skin deep, but the truth?
Your glow starts long before the medical-grade serum sinks in.

Because the real difference between radiant and run-down isn't the price of your skincare; it's how you treat yourself when no one's watching.
It's choosing rest over revenge scrolling.
It's saying no without guilt.
It's knowing that SPF protects your face, but boundaries protect your peace.

You can't fake the kind of glow that comes from peace, purpose, and properly fed hormones.
That's why this next part isn't about products; it's about presence.
So before you buy another brightening mask, take this as your reminder:
You don't need to chase radiance; you cultivate it.

Welcome to your next evolution, where *self-care meets self-respect,* and your routine becomes a ritual for the woman you're becoming.

Next Chapter: The Glow & Grow Guide
Because your relationship with yourself sets the tone for every other love story in your life.

"If they're not adding to your peace, your glow, or your collagen levels, let them go."

Your Glow and Grow Toolkit

Because your relationship with yourself sets the tone for every other love story in your life.

1. The Glow Routine – For Skin and Soul

Morning: Protect Your Peace
- Hydrate- with water and gratitude.
- Apply SPF to your face and your boundaries.
- Set one intention: "I will respond, not react."

Midday: Reapply Your Energy
- Take a walk, breathe, stretch, scroll less.
- Repeat your affirmation: "I attract calm, not chaos."
- Text your best friend, not your ex.

Evening: Cleanse & Release
- Take off your makeup and your emotional armour.
- Journal: What did I learn about myself today?
- Forgive yourself for not being perfect; you're evolving, not exfoliating.

2. The Growth Habits – Building Love That Lasts
Love doesn't just arrive; it grows where it's watered.

Here's your self-love watering schedule:

* * *

Daily: Say something kind to yourself. Out loud. Bonus points if it feels cringey; that means it's working.
Weekly: Do one thing that brings joy just for you, not for productivity or someone else's approval.
Monthly: Check in with your goals. Are they still yours, or have you absorbed someone else's expectations again?
Seasonally: Reflect. What's blossomed? What needs pruning? What's ready to be planted next?

Because growth isn't always pretty, sometimes it's messy, sweaty, tear-streaked, and uncomfortable. But that's how roots deepen.

3. The Emotional SPF Checklist

Before you let someone into your world, or your DMs, ask yourself: Do I feel safe expressing my needs?
Do I like who I am when I'm with them?
Do they add calm or chaos?
Do I feel seen, or just followed?
Am I choosing this connection, or chasing validation?

If it burns, blisters, or leaves you anxious, it's not love. It's emotional sun damage.

4. Feed Your Glow: Nourish to Flourish

Because love might feed the soul, but a good meal feeds the mood.

You can't manifest a healthy relationship on an empty stomach. You can journal all day about boundaries and Venus energy, but if you've had three coffees and a croissant since 9 a.m., your inner goddess is running on fumes.
Self-care isn't bubble baths and breath work, it's blood sugar

management.
Glowing skin, stable moods, and good dating decisions all start with one truth: you can't pour from an empty stomach.

Batch Cook Mondays: The Love Language of Future You

This is the one where I make my mum proud!
I'll be honest, I was a ping meal queen, quick, convenient and couldn't be arsed!
But I decided to level it up, and a few Sunday morning watches of certain cooking programmes gave me that next level up! (I guess I will eagerly await my invite onto James Martin's Saturday morning kitchen, to show off my batch cooking wins!)
My cooking abilities have evolved much like myself!

From cheese on toast to hearty cottage pie and homemade lasagnes.
After all, it is basically just another form of chemistry to master!
Mondays can be chaos, inboxes, commutes, existential dread.
But Batch Cook Mondays?
That's your love letter to the rest of the week.
Think of it as meal prepping for your peace of mind.
You're not just saving time and money, you're nourishing your nervous system.

How to do it:
Set the vibe, music on (try my playlist!), hair up, maybe a glass of wine.
You're not just "meal prepping"; you're hosting Hot Girl with a Saucepan.

Cook three base dishes: a protein, agrain, and a rainbow tray of roasted veggies.
***

Or you could utilise something like a lean beef, turkey or quorn mince and smash out a huge slow cooker medley of spaghetti bolognaise or chilli con carne in the colder months.
In the summer, a super salad goes a long way.

Mix and match all week, freeze some for a lazy day.

Add a self-care snack for joy in an edible form.
One of my faves is rice cakes, banana and peanut butter, or homemade mini egg bites in my air fryer! Another go-to is a wholesome granola and yoghurt, berry mix.

Eat As You Love Yourself

It's not about dieting, it's about devotion.
Every meal sends a message: "I care enough about myself to keep myself nourished."
Hydrate like it's your part-time job.
And don't skip meals for men, meetings, or manicures.
Balanced hormones = balanced dating decisions.
No one finds their soulmate hangry.

Cowgirl Era: Ride Your Own Damn Horse

They say healing looks like journaling, bubble baths, and green juice. But sometimes? Healing looks like blasting Beyoncé in your kitchen, wearing boots that could kick a bad habit straight into next week, and finally, choosing yourself.

The Cowgirl Era isn't about being reckless; it's about rediscovering your spark.
It's the moment you swap codependency for country playlists, and remember that the only person who needs to ride in and save you…
is you.

***

Friends might joke that I've been a matador in love, always running toward red flags like they're designer handbags on sale. But this era? It's about slowing down, noticing the signs, and deciding that peace is sexier than chaos.

So go ahead, throw on your boots, grab your confidence (and maybe a vino), and gallop into your next chapter.

This is your Cowgirl Era: wild, wise, and finally all about you.

137

Reflection The Cowgirl Commandments

Because you can't gallop into your glow-up without checking your saddle (and your standards).

***

What red flags am I still drawn to and why?
What songs make me feel powerful, grounded, and myself again?
(Check out my playlist for the ones I go to that have helped me
write this book!)
Where am I still chasing validation instead of joy?

What would "peace" look like if it wore boots and confidence?
How can I honour my independence and my softness at the same
time? Write it, sing it, or shout it in your kitchen, whatever you do,
make it yours.

5. Body Love & Movement

(Because your body isn't a project, it's a partner.)

Movement isn't punishment; it's a celebration.
When you move with love, you shift your energy.

You stop living from your head and start living from your hips.

Dance, stretch, walk, breathe or head to the gym; however you
move, make it joy-driven, not guilt-driven.

Move for Mood, Not Metrics:

- Morning stretch with coffee.
- Kitchen dancing while batch cooking.
- Long walks with a podcast that makes you snortlaugh.
- Yoga, pilates, lifting, swimming, anything that makes your body
say "thank you," not "why?"

Confidence isn't a look, it's an energy. And energy starts in motion.

6.Paws & Presence: Loving Through Pet Care

(Because sometimes the best relationship you'll ever have has fur, a wagging tail, and zero mixed signals.)

There's something deeply healing about welcoming a pet into your world. It's love stripped of ego, words, and "what are we?" conversations.

It's pure connection, built on routine, trust, and gentle consistency. When you care for an animal, you learn the quiet art of showing up. You feed them, walk them, talk to them in ridiculous voices and somewhere in between, you realise:

This is what healthy love feels like.

No mixed signals.
No ghosting.

Just loyalty, presence, and a lot of fur on your black jeans.

The Early Days: Building Trust

Just like dating, the first few weeks with a new pet are about reading cues, establishing rhythm, and earning trust.
Only this time, the communication is beautifully simple: a tail wag, a slow blink, a soft purr.

Here's the secret: animals mirror your energy.
When you're calm, they relax.
When you're anxious, they sense it.
They remind you that love doesn't have to be loud; it just has to be consistent.

Self-Care Through Pet Care

Caring for a pet naturally builds habits that strengthen you:

- **Routine.** You feed, walk, or play at set times and that rhythm grounds you more than any productivity app ever could.
- **Mindfulness.** You can't doom-scroll when a pair of big eyes is staring at you, waiting for affection or dinner.
- **Compassion.** You learn patience and softness, especially on the days when you don't feel like showing up for anyone, including yourself.
- **Touch & comfort**. There's therapy in a cuddle session with something small, furry, and totally judgment-free.

It's self-soothing but with fur and emotional support noises.

Healing in Motion

If you've been through heartbreak or loneliness, animals help rebuild your sense of safety in connection.
They remind you it's okay to trust again, that love can be safe, steady, and wordless.

Taking your dog for a walk becomes movement and mindfulness. Brushing your cat becomes meditation. Caring for them becomes caring for you.

They don't care how you look, what you earn, or who texted back. They just need your time and tenderness, and isn't that what we all really want?

***

Reflection: The Pet Care = Self-Care Ritual

Because looking after another living thing, even a small, biscuit-obsessed one, teaches you more about love than any dating app ever could.

Take a moment to reflect:

How do I show up for my pet, even on the days I don't feel my best?
What has my pet taught me about patience or routine?
How do I comfort my pet, and how can I offer myself that same care? What boundaries do I keep for their well-being, and can I mirror those for myself?
What does unconditional love look like in my world?

Self-Care Check-In:

- ☑ I'm feeding myself nourishing meals.
- ☑ I'm creating small, grounding routines.
- ☑ I'm resting when I need to recharge.
- ☑ I'm speaking to myself with kindness.
- ☑ I'm giving love without abandoning myself.

The Gentle Close: What Your Pet Already Knows

Caring for your pet isn't a chore; it's a daily reminder that love grows through consistency, not perfection.
When you feed them, you nurture. When you walk them, you ground. When you love them, you heal.
And maybe that's the lesson this whole book has been whispering all along: the tenderness you give so freely belongs to you, too.
So go ahead, pour the cat biscuits, light a candle, and whisper to your cat (or dog, or goldfish):

"We're doing great."
Because you are.

Next Chapter Teaser:
As you master the art of loving yourself, fur, flaws and all, it's time
to look toward what comes next: love without losing yourself.
*But just before all that, I want to share the playlist that has inspired
this book.*

* * *

Welcome to the **End Game** — where independence meets
intimacy, and self-worth ecomes your ultimate love language.

Venus, Mars and Vino

"Warning: This playlist may cause kitchen dancing, confidence and sudden clarity about why he wasn't the one."

Playlists to power up and LOVE yourself!

https://www.tunemymusic.com/share/TwOqJ5TSrV

Available on all music platforms

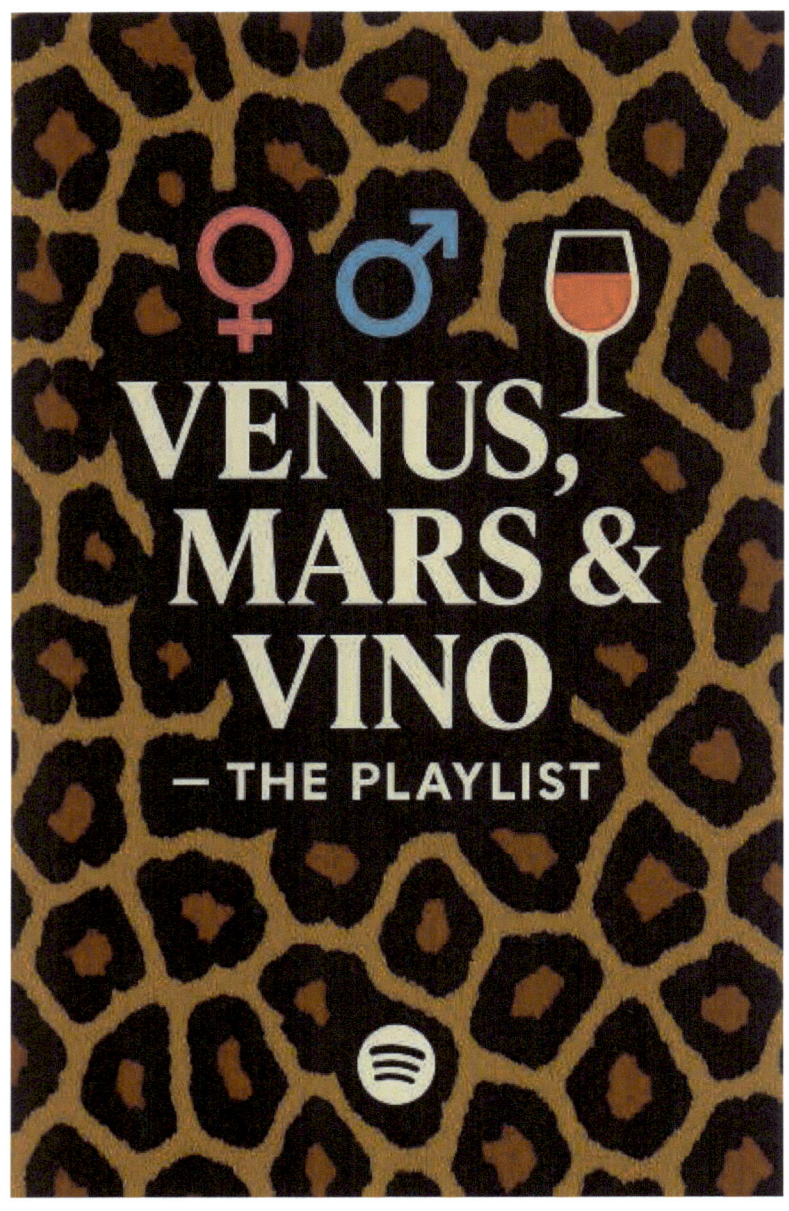

"The real end game isn't finding someone, it's finding yourself, and refusing to lose her again."

The End Game: Love Without Losing Yourself

The Real Markers of a Healthy Relationship

Forget the fairy tales, a healthy relationship doesn't look like constant fireworks. It's more like a steady flame that burns warm, not wild.

It's not passion or peace, it's both, in harmony.

Here's what real love looks like (and what Instagram doesn't show you):

1. Safety over spark.
You feel calm, not anxious. You can express yourself without fear of being judged, rejected, or gaslit.

2. Curiosity, not control.
You ask questions because you care, not because you're checking up.
You want to understand, not own.

3. Effort, not excuses.
Healthy love requires maintenance, check-ins, kindness, and accountability.
You water it, even when it rains.

4. Repair over-perfection. Disagreements aren't disasters.
You both know how to apologise, communicate, and reconnect.
***

5.Freedom within togetherness.
You don't have to shrink to fit each other's needs. You grow, individually and together.
Real love isn't about never fighting; it's about fighting fairly. It's not about constant butterflies; it's about consistent peace.

If love makes you smaller, it's not love, it's ego dressed as romance.

How to Keep Your Independence While in Love

Here's the catch: when we fall in love, we often merge.
Our playlists, our plans, our personalities start to blur into this cute little "we," and suddenly, "I" becomes an endangered species.

But keeping your independence isn't selfish, it's essential.
It's the glue that holds your identity together when life gets messy.
Here's how to stay you, even when you're part of an "us":

Keep your solo rituals- Morning coffee, solo walks, reading time, don't abandon the habits that make you, YOU.

Maintain your friendships- Your partner shouldn't replace your social circle. Keep your people close; they're your emotional GPS.
The Spice Girls taught us that…"If you wanna be my lover…"

Have separate goals- A shared vision is beautiful, but you both need individual ambitions that light you up.

Communicate needs, not fears- Independence doesn't mean emotional distance, it means owning your emotions, not outsourcing them.
***

Check your boundaries- Healthy love says, "I choose to share my life with you," not, "I need you to complete it."

Because the strongest relationships are two whole people choosing to walk side by side, not two halves trying to fill a void.

The Difference Between "Finding Love" and "Choosing Love!"

Finding love is chemistry, sparks, attraction, and timing. Choosing love is commitment, effort, grace, and growth.

You can find love a hundred times in your life.
But choosing it? That's the magic.

Finding love is the start of a story.
Choosing love is showing up every day to write the next chapter.

It's staying curious when it's easier to judge.
It's being honest when it's tempting to avoid.
It's forgiving when you could walk away.

Choosing love means you don't rely on fate; you build it, brick by emotional brick.

Love Without Losing Yourself

Here's the beautiful paradox: when you love from wholeness, not hunger, you don't lose yourself, you expand.
You stop asking, "Who am I in this relationship?" And start asking, "Who am I becoming through this love?"

True love doesn't dim your light; it reflects it back to you. It says, "I see you. Stay you."

***

The endgame isn't about being perfectly in sync.
It's about being perfectly authentic, two souls choosing each other, again and again, without erasing who they are in the process.

So here's the real secret: writing this book and getting the thoughts out of my head has actually taught me things, too. I have been on this very journey with you.

You don't need to chase love, perform for it, or prove you deserve it.
You are love.
You always were.

And when you remember that, when you date, flirt, and fall from that place of fullness, you'll never lose yourself again.

Because the greatest love story you'll ever live isn't the one where someone chooses you.
It's the one where you choose yourself… and let someone worthy meet you there.

Because here's the truth no one tells you: even when you've mastered love without losing yourself, you still need to maintain your glow, inside and out.

Healthy relationships are built on self-respect, but great skin helps too. And while you can't control who texts you back, you can control your self-care, SPF, hydration, and emotional boundaries.

So before we wrap up your romantic renaissance, let's talk about something just as important as love languages and emotional intelligence: your self-care strategy.
Whether it's protecting your heart or your skin barrier, the principle is the same:
***

Always wear protection, SPF for the sun, and boundaries for the red flags.

Who knows where the journey will end, at least we have (some) idea now of where to start, and I don't think I am done telling my stories yet.....

Yours Truly

Annette Matthews
Aka: The Matador

"If love is a gamble, at least now I know how to stop betting on clowns. Cheers to that."

Epilogue

Here's what I want you to remember:

You are not hard to love.
You just needed to love yourself enough not to settle for half-versions of it.

You are not behind.
You are building something sustainable.

You are not too much.
You just haven't met someone yet who's fluent in your language.

And most importantly, your glow-up isn't a phase. It's your baseline now.

Keep choosing you

Keep choosing the quiet mornings, the therapy sessions, the boundaries, and the good food.
Keep choosing laughter, curiosity, and the kind of love that doesn't make you anxious.
Keep choosing SPF for your skin and your sanity.
I've learnt even more about myself by sharing this book with you, my readers, so a heartfelt thanks to anyone who bought, shared, or gifted this.

Because choosing yourself doesn't mean you've given up on love.
It means you *finally* understand what kind of love is worth your energy.
***

And if you ever forget...

Go back to your rituals.
Make your Batch Cook Monday magic.
Dance in your kitchen.
Scream in the woods. (Seriously, try this) Watch a strong princess Disney icon
Watch The Holiday on TV (even if it's July!)
Remind yourself just how bad Bridget Jones had it! (She has her iconic new statue on Leicester Square, go check it out!)
Write your own full-moon intentions.
Look in the mirror and say,

"I am the love story."
Because you are, every healed, hilarious, heart-on-fire cowgirl hat-wearing, part of you.

In closing...

Here's to you, the woman who stopped waiting to be chosen and started choosing herself.

To the one who knows that love is sweeter when it's peaceful, that skincare is self-respect, and that red flags are not decoration.

Here's to your next chapter, whatever and whoever it holds, may it be honest, joyful, and completely yours.

Now go live it. Glowing. Growing. Unapologetically you.

SPF on.
Standards high.
Heart open.
Shining always.

Acknowledgements

To my readers

You're the reason this exists.
You're the proof that we can talk about love, boundaries, and moon cycles and still have a wicked sense of humour about it all.
You turned this from a scribbled idea into a shared conversation, one skinny flat white, one vino, one heartbreak, one healed boundary at a time.

To my friends

Thank you for being you. You know who you are.
You've seen me through pretty much everything in meme and real-life forms.
You are the Venus to my Mars, the SPF to my red flags, and the reason I still believe in good people (and good wine, paired with cheese).

To my family

Thank you for your patience, encouragement, and ability to pretend that every story in this book is "fictional."
You've been my foundation, my reality check, and my constant reminder that love in all its forms starts at home.
My Daughter, Lois, has and always will be my wingman and the reason why I do what I do. For her and for us.
My world, our world, absolutely our oyster!

***

To the healers, heartbreakers, and holy messes I've met along the way

You were all teachers.
Some taught me kindness, some taught me lessons, and a few taught me the value of blocking early.
You've all contributed to this story, whether you know it or not.
(And no, I will not be naming names) Not worth the airtime!

And finally, to you, again

For daring to do the work.
For choosing to heal instead of harden.
For protecting your peace, your skin barrier, and your sense of humour.
You are the proof that love, real love, begins the moment you decide to stop settling and start shining.

Here's to you.
Here's to us.
Here's to love without losing yourself.

Now go Shine on!

References & Inspirations

References & Inspirations

While Venus, Mars & Vino is built on my lived experience, humour, heartbreaks, healed energy, and a decade of conversations with women, the following themes, thinkers, and cultural touch points helped shape and inspire the messages in this book. This list honours the ideas, concepts, and cultural references that influenced the journey, not because the content is copied, but because modern love is a shared language we're all still learning.

Books & Writers Who Inspired the Conversation
• Men Are from Mars, Women Are from Venus - John Grey (referenced in tone + playful gender dynamics). Thanks, Mum, for buying me this!
• Attached -Amir Levine & Rachel Heller (inspiration for the attachment styles chapter)
• Brené Brown- vulnerability, boundaries & emotional courage
• Esther Perel- modern desire, relational intelligence
• Anna Williamson -conversational, accessible dating advice tone
• Dolly Alderton- modern dating, honesty and humour ("Everything I Know About Love")
• Florence Given — self-worth, feminism, boundaries
• Mel Robbins- Let them
• Cara Alwill- Girl on Fire
• Jo Malone- My Story
• Woman- Jodie Salt
• Love Your Skin- Nicci Leigh
• Let's Do This- Richard Branson
• Atomic Habits- James Clear
• Why Mummy's Sloshed- Gill Sims

- *Do It Like a Woman- Caroline Criado-Perez*
- *The Imposter Cure- Dr Jeremy Hibberd*
- *How to leave your psychopath- Maddy Anholt (Thank you to Christina and Jolene for the advice on reading this lady's amazing but sad story)*

Pop Culture / Characters Referenced
- *Sex and the City - witty female friendships, dating chaos, humour*
- *Bridget Jones - self-deprecating, warm British humour*
- *Disney Heroines - Moana, Pocahontas, Belle (independent woman reframing)*
- *The Holiday- Sassy Cameron Diaz and a heartbroken Kate Winslet in one of their best!*

Astrological + Cosmic Influences
- *Classical zodiac archetypes (public domain concepts)*
- *Modern astrology tropes from popular culture (moon phases, star-sign behaviours)*

Psychological & Relationship Frameworks
- *The Big Five Personality Traits (public domain psychological model)*
- *Love Languages- Gary Chapman (acknowledging inspiration only)*
- *Domestic Violence Disclosure Scheme (Claire's Law) -UK Government/ Police guidance*
- *Healthy relationship markers derived from common therapeutic models (e.g., CBT, attachment theory, trauma-informed anecdotals*

Themes Drawn From Everyday Culture
- *Modern dating app terminology (ghosting, bread crumbing, love bombing, etc.) is a widely used digital culture vocabulary*
- *Social media influence on dating standards*

Venus, Mars and Vino

- *Feminine wellness trends (self-care routines, glow-up culture)*
- *Body positivity and self-image movements*
- *Spotify playlists, soundtracks & musical culture used as mood inspiration*

Personal Experience & Observations
With special thanks to Thames valley police force
Much of this book is shaped by:
- *real-life dating experiences*
- *conversations with friends*
- *stories anonymous women have shared over the years*
- *the relatable chaos of modern relationships*
- *professional grounding as a dental hygienist & Therapist (health, care, wellbeing themes)*
- *Motherhood, Single parenting and identity evolution*

These experiences form the heart of Venus, Mars & Vino, keeping it honest, warm, human, and rooted in lived truth.

Design & Aesthetic Inspiration
- *Leopard print feminine branding (90s + modern resurgence)*
- *Cosmic colours and motifs (super moon, Venus energy)*
- *Editorial-style infographics and self-help toolkits*
- *Digital note-style "text screen" imagery (inspired by iMessage UI)*

Musical Influence
While all song titles belong to their respective artists, the emotional tone from Beyoncé, Lizzo, Taylor Swift, Florence + The Machine, Carrie Underwood, and Moana's soundtrack, to name just a few, helped inspire the book's energy, resilience, and feminine empowerment themes.

" This woman is fearless. I've known her for less than two years, yet it feels like I've known her my whole life. She's one of a kind, the sort of person whose presence fills a room and whose story you could never forget. Honestly, she's the only person I can imagine writing a book I'd actually want to read. Excited at what's to come"

Jessica
Fellow Wine drinker, Glamour queen, partner in crime, Hair guru and another one of my part-time therapists!

About the Author

Annette Matthews is a Dental Hygienist & Therapist, Skincare & Aesthetic Specialist, journalism student, and modern love survivor, the perfect cocktail of science, soul, and story behind Venus, Mars & Vino. Whether she's transforming smiles, restoring skin confidence, or writing with wit and emotional truth, Annette brings depth, humour, and heart to everything she touches.

Her daughter, **Lois**, is her greatest inspiration, a daily reminder that resilience can be soft, reinvention can be joyful, and SPF is both a skincare essential and a metaphor for boundaries.

Annette has survived a move-for-a-man catastrophe worthy of its own Netflix special, a red-flag roster that could fill a textbook, and enough ghosting to justify calling in a medium. Through it all, she discovered the message woven through this book:

You cannot control who leaves, lies, or lets you down, but you can control your glow, your growth, and who gets access to your heart.

When she's not creating healthy smiles or glowing skin, she's studying journalism, writing with unapologetic honesty, and turning her lived experience into guidance for women who are ready to stop chasing love and start choosing it.

Venus, Mars & Vino is her invitation to date smarter, heal deeper, laugh loudly, and remember that self-worth is the sexiest thing you can wear.

* * *

Because if Annette has learned one thing on this wild journey, it's this: **Sometimes, the real happily-ever-after is the woman you become on the way.**

Follow Annette for more real talk, self-care rituals, and cosmic humour:
Instagram: @annette_matthews_insta
Contact: Annette@leopardink.uk

Because loving yourself is the plot twist the dating world didn't see coming.

* * *

A Note from the Author

Responsible Drinking

Yes, there's wine all over these pages…but trust me, I don't drink enough to text an ex, buy a pony, or fall in love with a man who says "I'm just really busy right now."

So here's the vibe:
Sip like a queen, not a cautionary tale.
Hydrate between glasses, eat something carby, and know when it's time to switch to water before your mascara starts doing interpretive dance.

Drink joyfully.
Drink sensibly.
And for the love of good decisions
Never drink past the point you'd still choose yourself.

If You Need Support…

This book is full of humour, healing, and heart, but real life can feel heavier than any chapter.

If you ever find yourself struggling, overwhelmed, or feeling alone, please reach out.
You deserve support, softness, and someone to listen, always.
Here are some trusted mental health charities and helplines that offer confidential help, guidance, and a safe space to talk:

UK Support

- **Samaritans- 116 123 (24/7)**

For anyone feeling low, lost, or overwhelmed.
Free, confidential, and always open.

- **Mind- mind.org.uk**

Advice, support, and resources for a wide range of mental health challenges.

- **CALM (Campaign Against Living Miserably)- thecalmzone.net | 0800 58 58 58**

Support for anyone feeling anxious, hopeless, or struggling with their mental well-being.

- **Women's Aid - womensaid.org.uk**

Help, safety information and support for anyone experiencing emotional or physical abuse.

- **NHS 111 (Option 2 for mental health)**

Local mental health crisis services across the UK.

For Anyone, Anywhere

If you're reading this outside the UK, please seek local mental health helplines, emergency services, or community charities in your area.
Support exists in every country, and you deserve to access it.

***

A Final Reminder

Needing help doesn't make you weak.
Reaching out makes you human.
And healing doesn't have to be done alone.

* * *

Your story matters.
Your voice matters.
You matter.

Images from the Memory Vault- now get to creating yours!

www.ingramcontent.com/pod-product-compliance
Lightning Source LLC
Chambersburg PA
CBHW040844120626
46547CB00001B/12